Three Novellas by
Malania E. Reynolds

🍒 THREE SKILLET

Fields of Grain, Reynolds, Malania E.

First Edition

 THREE SKILLET

www.ThreeSkilletPublishing.com

Cover design by Farley L Dunn

All characters are fictitious, and any resemblance to actual persons living or dead is purely coincidental.

This book may not be reproduced in whole or in part, by electronic process or any other means, without permission of the author.

ISBN: 978-1-943189-35-9

Copyright © 2017 by Malania E. Reynolds

All Rights Reserved

Fields of grain

Chandler's Store

— 1 —

I remember well the first time I saw Rudolph Chandler.

One of the ranch hands returned from a weekend of riotous behavior in town and told my parents about a new store opened the previous month. Mother, of course, wanted to go and see the articles for sale right away, but Father told her it would be better to wait until Saturday when he could go with her. Mother had received last Christmas a letter from her sister in Mississippi about new gadgets for sale back East. She especially wanted some pins and needles that she badly needed for her sewing projects, and hoped the new storekeeper had them in stock.

On Saturday, before the sun was high in the eastern sky, we all piled into the wagon and headed the ten miles to town. Being small children, my brother and I were lying on quilts in the back, while Mother held baby sister in her arms. The ride was soothing, and I was soon fast asleep.

It was quite an adventure of itself to travel into town. Usually one of the hands or Father bought the few meager supplies to be had there. Twice a year, Father made a trip to the Army post at Fort Sill and brought back enough staples, like ground corn meal, flour, sugar and salt, to last the ranch until the next time. Occasionally, a wagon train or peddler would pass our way, Mother would "uh and ah" at the things for sale, and Father would buy her a new frying pan and cloth for new clothes or some canned goods.

Mostly, our ranch could supply all our needs. The cook, Old Pete, had a vegetable garden behind his one-room shanty. The seeds came from a supply house back East. He tended it with loving care, and most times, if Old Pete wasn't out in the garden hoeing his vegetables, he could be found peeling tons of potatoes or baking an endless supply of bread for the ranch hands. Our meat was beef or chickens. It was Mother's job to tend the chickens and collect the eggs. Now that I had reached the great age of six years, she let me help her, but I was secretly afraid of the red rooster, so sometimes pretended not to hear her when she asked if I wanted to help gather the eggs.

We also had a milk cow, because Mother said small children needed lots of milk. The cow's name was Lila. I loved the smell and taste of warm milk straight from Lila's teats. There were a few stray cats that had wandered to the ranch and hung around the barn at milking time. Father wanted to get rid of them, but Mother said they were handy at keeping the mice and rats from the barn.

Father had first journeyed to the Territory after the War Between the States. He had seen the rich soil and tall native grasses blowing in the breeze and determined to return. And, so he did. He sold his farm in Mississippi, gathered Mother, us kids and all their possessions into a large wagon and set out with several other families to "settle in the West." My brother Richard hadn't been born yet, Thomas was almost six and my sister Rose was a babe in arms. I was about three years old when we first laid claim to the land that's now one the largest ranches in the Territory.

Indians were sometimes a bother, begging for food or

stealing beef from the open range if that suited them better. Mother always gave them bread or meat when they came to the house. She made several quilts to distribute during the hard winters. They went back and forth from the open range to Fort Sill. The soldiers tried to protect the settlers as best they could. Sometimes shots were fired from angry Indians or settlers, and some people were killed, but mostly the savages were peaceful in our area.

On this particular morning in late July, the sun rose high into the sky and the heat under our blanket became uncomfortable, so Thomas and I sat up and began to look around for familiar landmarks. I could see we were coming into the outskirts of town. There were the livery stable and the blacksmith's home on the left.

It wasn't much of a town in those days. It had been a lone trading post on the prairie where the local ranchers gathered to talk politics and weather. When the old trader died, the large log building was left vacant. A few saloons and outhouses sprang up next to the trading post. There was a lawyer's shack, occupied by Mr. Delano Jones, who was drunk most of the time, Mother said.

Mrs. Alice Jennings, daughter of the trader and a widow with two small children, lived in the only real house in town. Her husband was a soldier and killed at Shiloh. She cooked and sewed clothes, mostly shirts, for the single cowboys or strangers traveling through the town. She and Mother visited together whenever we ventured into town, and sometimes spent the night when the weather caught us too far from home to travel.

She was a jolly woman, quick with laughter, and a somewhat crude manner, but had a kind word for everyone she met. Her daughters were twins, Caroline and Evelyn, several years older than I. The girls and I got along well, and I enjoyed the company of girls to play with, for all that I was more accustomed to the men on the ranch.

I could see as we approached the trader's log building that it was no longer vacant. A huge sign hung across the front and under the roof that announced in black letters, Chandler's Store. Underneath in smaller print, the sign said, Groceries and Sundries; Hardware and Guns. The two windows had recently been cleaned and reflected the morning sunshine. The door stood open, and I could see several people going in or out.

Father stopped the team in front of the store. He tied the reins on the hitching rail, helped Mother from the wagon and handed baby Rose to her. He turned to us. Thomas and I jumped into his waiting arms. We went as a group into the store.

My first impression was of the pleasing aroma that drifted from the supplies scattered all about; spices and tobacco mixed with garlic and dust teased my nostrils with abandon. As my eyes grew accustomed to the darkness, I could see new shelves built along the walls and filled with canned goods. Open barrels holding corn, flour, beans and sour pickles lined the center aisle. Shelves built clear to the ceiling contained multicolored bolts of cloths, and factory-made clothing hung on pegs in one corner.

From around the counter walked a giant of a man, with black hair slightly curling around his ears, and a booming voice that seemed to come from somewhere deep in his belly. There was a scar on his face that extended from his temple and hairline down to his chin, leaving him with an angry, scowling look. A dark mole sat on the right side of his mouth, and the shadow of a beard that had recently been shaved gave his face a dark color.

It was the first time I remember being frightened in my life.

As he approached our group, I ducked behind my mother's skirts, hoping he wouldn't see me. He shook hands and introduced himself to Father in that loud rumble and turned to my mother. I quivered with fear as I saw his eyes lowered to Thomas and me standing beside her.

"Hello, and who is this?" I closed my eyes tight and clung to my mother. She tried to gently bring me forward to be introduced, but I held back, covering myself with her long skirts, using them like a shield against this huge man. "Well, no hurry," he said, "We'll get to know each other in time." As he turned away to talk to Father, I slowly opened my eyes and saw my mother's face, shame and embarrassment at my impolite behavior clearly visible in her eyes.

She turned and walked away, leaving me alone in the middle of the floor. Thomas trailed after her. Father and Big Man were talking beside the pot-bellied stove as though they'd been friends for years. I stood a moment trying to decide what to do without my family support. I heard a giggle from behind a barrel. It was Caroline Jennings, whom I had previously considered my friend. Her mother stood near the sewing notions counter, looking at a jar of mixed buttons.

"What are you afraid of?" she asked, laughing the whole time. "You've seen men before."

And, it was true. Living on the ranch as we did, I'd seen probably a hundred men come and go, tall and short, slim and fat. But, there was something about Mr. Chandler that sent chills down my back and made my fingers curl in fear. I sneaked a small peek at him across the room, just as he glanced my way. His dark eyebrows raised in question; his left eye above the scar slowly dropped into a wink; and I almost died right there on the spot. I didn't look at him again the entire hour we were in his store. I took in every smell and every sight, so that I can clearly see it today, as I write these words as an old woman.

I gaily talked to Caroline about the new school term, and the new boys in town who would be in our school, but not once did I approach my mother or father as they gathered the supplies and talked to the townspeople who drifted in and out of the store.

Just as we began to leave the store, an amazing thing happened. Suddenly, right in front of my breast, there was a large brown hand holding a stick of cherry-flavored hard candy, my favorite kind. I looked up, and there was the scar-faced giant not a foot from me, with a peace offering. I ignored the candy and ran from the store, as though all the ghosts from the cemetery were after me. I dashed to the wagon, hopped into the back and hid under the quilts. Through the thick folds, I could hear Mother and Father talking about their first visit to Chandler's Store, satisfied with their purchases as we left the town behind. Finally, I lifted my head from the quilt and looked back. Dust rose in our wake as we moved along. And through the dust, I could just make out the shape of a man standing in the street looking after us.

— 2 —

I saw Rudy Chandler many times in the following years, and a profile of his past began to take shape, along with the identities of the rest of the inhabitants of the town. He had a large family in Virginia. He'd lived on a plantation that was destroyed and burned by the Yankee soldiers. His father owned slaves and died during the war. His mother married again and moved to Richmond. His four sisters were married and had produced many children. Two of his brothers perished in the war. Two brothers had gone to California and another brother lived in Arkansas.

Mr. Chandler had been in the Confederate Cavalry, injured and captured in Mississippi, and sent to Delaware as a prisoner of war. He spent two years in appalling conditions before being exchanged and sent home. It was in the prison camp that he determined if he survived, he'd go west and operate a store. He told Father that he wanted to make a new beginning where there were no bitter memories to remind him of his old life. Father told Mother he couldn't blame him for that, for it was exactly what he himself had done.

Mr. Chandler went back to Virginia once a year to

visit, usually early in spring, to see his family and make purchases for his store. The supplies would come in a wagon train along with more settlers for the surrounding area and town. We were in town one day when I was about twelve years old, when the supplies arrived. I remember my mother's excitement that day. Mr. Chandler had promised her the latest style in a hat. I'll never forget the look on her face when she opened the round box tied with blue ribbon that he handed to her. Out of the box came the most gorgeous straw bonnet that ever existed, with snow-white egret plumes and long blue ribbons to tie under the neck. Mother wore that hat at every opportunity, and Father would treat her with great pomp and respect when she wore it.

I was growing into a tall, gangly young woman. I'm not beautiful of face as my sister Rose became. My eyes and hair are brown, but sometimes it became streaked with gold when out in the summer sun. My skin, too often, was brown and peeling from the relentless sun, when I forgot to wear my hat. Some of the ladies in town said I'd amount to nothing because I was so wild. In a way, it was true. Living on the ranch, I rode my horse every day, and often helped with the cattle. Mother tried her best to make a lady out of me, using her Southern gentlewoman background to encourage and inspire me. I roamed over the prairie and gullies as though they belonged to only me. Several times I came upon Indians or strange men, but I was never frightened. I knew I could outride anyone on my mare, Nellie. I could rope strays and shoot as well as anyone on the ranch. I could shoe a horse or castrate a bull.

I finished my eighth year of schooling and thought that was enough. Mother and Father discussed sending me back East to stay with my mother's sister, Katherine. I began to dream of being a grand lady as Mother had once been with all the men at my feet and the other girls fainting with envy. I used my brothers, Thomas and Richard, shamelessly to try out my dancing steps and flirting ways.

We sat quietly listening as Mother described the old days under the Southern sky with the black people working in the fields, and she, sitting on the veranda, a cool drink in hand, talking and laughing with the neighbors. She spoke of the huge balls where the ladies wore fancy pastel dresses, and the gentlemen courted them with flowers and jeweled fans. The fox hunting and manly sports competitions appealed to Thomas much more than the long hot days of enticing stray cattle out of hidden bushes or draws.

It wasn't so much the soft Southern nights or the soirees that appealed to me as the traveling itself. Oh, how I longed to see the tall cottonwoods, red oaks and elms, and smell the magnolias. There were no trees to speak of in the Territory. Maybe, a few spindly mesquites or cedars grew along the riverbanks, but not the huge forests of my parents' day. I could barely remember them, and the memory was fading along with my early days spent on the plantation.

Thomas at fourteen was already taller than I. His face was chapped and red from the sun. His hands were dark and strong like Father's. He went to school half a day but hated it. He sometimes whined and complained about the long hours of toil and sweat, but I thrived on it. He secretly drank and gambled with the ranch hands in the bunkhouse, and Father knew. Father told Mother when she spoke of it that all boys had to learn.

Rose was beautiful but lazy. She seemed to always be in her room brushing her hair or admiring herself in the only mirror in the house. She sat reading the few newspapers we received and ordered books from a supply house back East. She never went out in the sunshine, even with a hat. When Mother asked for help in the kitchen, she found something important to do right away. Even after a hard day riding out with the men, I'd be called on to do kitchen work or the laundry. I tried not to mind, because Mother worked hard, too, and she was a real lady.

My brother, Richard, was born on the ranch, four years after Rose. He was always shy and spindly. The doctor said he needed to get out more in the sunshine, so Father taught him to ride and fish and hunt. But, he was never as good at staying on a horse as I was. He drowned in the swimming hole when I was fifteen. They buried him on the ridge behind the barn, and we mourned him, for we loved him dearly.

In my seventeenth year, disaster struck the ranch. First, my mother came down with the influenza, and although the new doctor from town was called, she died on the fifth night of her illness. She was buried beside my brother Richard, behind the barn. A wooden fence was erected and whitewashed to help protect the grave from stray animals. Father was shaken and seemed for a while not to want to go on with life. The work of the ranch and barn fell to Thomas and the hired hands. Rose went into deep mourning, and her beautiful face was often marred by her tearstained cheeks and red eyes. I took over the kitchen chores and lost the freedom I had known wandering the fields and working with the cattle and horses.

There was little rain that spring, and the creeks and cattle tanks were low. The men carried buckets of water from the well during the long summer months to water the herd. The grass started out green but quickly turned brown, and the last of the winter hay was needed to supplement the feeding. The fall roundup was smaller than it had been for many years, and Father decided to sell a larger amount to strengthen the herd. We thought the winter snows and rain would help the grass to recover from the drought, but it became even worse. The warm, dry air quickly killed the remaining native grass, and we were forced to buy hay from the neighbors, who were really no better off than we were.

The second winter brought even more problems as storm after storm hit. The snow was welcome to water the fields, but the biting winds and freezing temperatures killed more cattle, and the chickens refused to lay their eggs. In the spring thaw, Father, Thomas, the cowboys and I rode the prairie and gullies, and for days the buzzards circled overhead. Father's alarm grew as more calves lay dead beside their mothers. A few calves were found alive and taken to the barn, where they were taught to nurse from a cow that had lost its calf. The shorthorn bull, Goliath, died that winter.

Father seemed to withdraw more into himself. He'd spent the greater part of his life building up the herd. He rode long hours on the prairie on his horse, checking the grass, green and lush from the moisture, but less than a hundred cattle were left to nibble it. Sometimes, I rode silently beside him. More often than not those days, I was left with the work of the household, sweeping, cooking, laundry and baking. I asked Rose to help, but she said she just couldn't, and would run to her room and cry some more.

One morning in early May, a few weeks before my nineteenth birthday, Father sat at breakfast with a sad look on his face. As though making a major decision, he looked at me and told me to meet him in his office. I left the table and followed him to the back room where he kept his papers on the cattle and men who worked for us.

"Jewel, I'm at my lowest point," he said, his voice low and sounding strangely humble to my ears. I can't remember my father ever speaking in such a way, before or since that day. "I can only think of one way out of the situation of the last few years. The grass is coming back, and there's water in the wells, but we need cattle to run a ranch. We'll need to keep the last of the herd separated for a while to see if they survive. What we need is new blood to start again, and a new bull. It's going to take money, a lot of money. I talked to Rudy Chandler last week when I was in town, and he made me a proposition. I'm sorry, darling, I've tried to come up with another way, but I just can't seem to think beyond today and what's needed to get this ranch going again." He sat for a moment looking at me in speculation. He rubbed his massive hands across his face as if that gesture would give him inspiration. Then, making his final decision, he said, "Girl, I'm asking a big sacrifice of you. Chandler offered to loan me money to buy new cattle and maybe dig a few more wells, so we won't ever have this kind of problem again when the drought hits. But, I'll need your cooperation in this venture."

"What is it, Pa?" I could see he was troubled, and I wanted to save him from worry. "What can I do to help?"

"Chandler offered to loan me the money, if you'll marry him," my father said, without looking at me.

"Marry him? Marry Mr. Chandler?" My voice was trembling, and I felt my stomach twist into knots. My whole body seemed to grow warm, a whisper of wind from the open window causing the hair on my neck to rise. "You want me to marry Rudy Chandler, the storekeeper?"

"It's the only way, girl." He wouldn't look me in the eyes. "I can't go to the bank; everyone in town will gossip and stare, probably laugh, too. The great James McLean, having to borrow money. If they find out how bad the situation is out here, the other ranchers and those damn farmers in the valley, too, I bet, will be coming around like vultures ready to pick over the pieces. God, I'll do almost anything before I'll let that happen."

I'd never heard my father talk with such a tone of sarcasm and wounded pride before. I looked more closely at the man sitting in front of me. Suddenly, I could see things about him I hadn't noticed before. His hair had turned gray. His eyes were no longer clear, but cloudy and red-rimmed, like Rose's had become in the last two years. Wrinkles had formed along his cheek line and around the corners of his eyes. My father's shoulders drooped, and he sat, gazing out the open window at the range that only last year had been dotted with cattle, but now was almost deserted. I remembered that he had let two of the hands go in the last month, Bob and Slim, two good, hard-working cattlemen.

I, too, looked out that window and thought how it was when I was small, with Mother baking in the kitchen, and Father sitting at the table, a big cigar in his mouth. Somehow, I thought my life would always be on the ranch. I knew that Thomas, being the eldest, would inherit, but surely there was a place for me here. I pictured myself out on the range, riding Nellie, with maybe a tall handsome husband beside me. The evenings would be spent sitting in front of the fire with my children about my knee.

Suddenly, the dream went away, and I could see another picture, Father and Mother and Rose gone, and Thomas with his wife and children. It would be his home, his ranch, and his children sitting by the fireplace. There was really no future for me on this land I loved. So, I decided to agree.

"Yes, Father," I said aloud. "If my marriage to Rudy Chandler is the best way to save the ranch, then I'll do it." My heart was thumping madly. My palms were sweating, so I rubbed them against my dress. I held my breath for his answer.

He turned and looked me in the eye for the first time since we entered the room. A great sigh filled his lungs and escaped through his lips. He burst from his chair as though he could no longer remain still and marched across the room. Relief was clear in every move. He stood for a moment at the window, his massive shoulders turned away from me. His whole manner of a few minutes before changed. He turned and lifted me from my chair, swung me high in his arms as though I were again three years old, and laughing with a mighty rumble deep in his chest, he set me down again.

"By God, girl, I didn't think you'd do it. I truly didn't think you'd agree," He sighed again. "Rudy Chandler, of all people, to be the husband of my little girl."

"Why, Father?" I was puzzled by his changed behavior, by the wonder in his voice.

"Why? I told you why, to save the ranch. I don't understand what you're asking me."

"Why did you think I wouldn't agree to the marriage?"

"Oh, you were always so afraid of him. I don't think you ever speak to him when we're in the store, do you? And, yet, you agreed to marry the man." He paused for a moment, his brow furrowed in thought. "You haven't changed your mind? You will go through with it? Because, I'll tell you the truth, darling, if I go to him and say you will and later you back out, I'll be angrier than I can say."

"I'll marry him, Father. I won't change my mind. You can write him an answer today, if you like."

"Good girl. I'll write him now. Go on out to the kitchen and bring me something to eat, for I tell you the truth, I didn't have much appetite the last few days, not knowing how to tell you of his offer." He turned to his desk drawer as if searching for paper.

I walked away a few steps, then turned and looked back. The man who had looked so old an hour ago now looked the same, but different. It was in his manner, his eyes now clear, his mouth smiling, his shoulders straightened and goodness me, he was whistling. I shook my head and left the room.

I filled a plate with biscuits and sausage and carried

them to him. He was sitting at his desk writing his letter to Mr. Chandler. He didn't look up or thank me, just grabbed for a biscuit from the plate. I left him there.

I filled the kettle with water and heated it to wash the breakfast dishes. Thomas had gone out to the barn. I could see him talking with one of the hands. I supposed that Rose had gone to her room to finish the book she'd started the night before. I stood alone staring out the window at the same scene that I had looked at most of my life: the barns and corrals with a couple of horses grazing on the tall grass, the chicken pens and the milk cow, Lila, contentedly chewing her cud. Everything seemed as it should be. I was the only one who had changed. In the course of one hour's time, my life had turned upside down and stretched hopelessly into the future. I no longer belonged here. I looked around the kitchen, my mother's kitchen. Now, Rose would cook and clean until Thomas married. I took a deep breath and sighed.

What did I know of Rudolph Chandler? Would he be a good husband? He was twenty years older than me. I remembered someone had mentioned years ago something about him. What was it? A picture of him arose in my mind, and I could see his face clearly, the scar standing out white against his dark skin; his gray eyes looking at me but not smiling.

I didn't remember him ever smiling at anyone. Laughing, yes, a couple of times I'd heard him laugh at one of the farmer's jokes, but never a spontaneous smile for his customers or for me. Suddenly, it came back, the memory of a rancher's wife saying that he'd had a lover once. A beautiful, Southern bride, who had promised to marry him, but when told he'd been injured and horribly scarred, she'd married another man. I thought how it must have been for him, far off in a Yankee prison dreaming of his home and family, of the girl waiting for his return. How he must have died inside when she hadn't waited. Was that why he was single at thirty-eight years old? Did he still think of his lover? Did he go to see her with her husband and children when he visited his family in Virginia?

Well, I'd promised to marry him. I couldn't change my mind. Father was at that moment writing a letter of acceptance of his bargain. The money would save the ranch and Father from ruin. Thomas would inherit the ranch and raise his family here. Rose would go away to school in the East instead of me. I would marry Rudy Chandler and become a storekeeper's wife and live in town forever.

A shudder ran through my body, and I turned to lift the kettle from the stove. I poured water into the basin and lowered the bar of soap, swishing to make suds. The water was too hot, and I burned my hand. I laughed. Served me right, I thought, for standing there dreaming when there was work to be done.

— 3 —

Two days later, I was thumping bread dough, sending flour rising in a cloud around me, when I heard a wagon roll into the yard. The dogs started howling. I grabbed a cloth and turned to the door as a knock sounded. I opened the door, and there, dressed in his somber dark blue suit, was Mr. Chandler.

"Miss McLean," he said.

Without thinking, I exclaimed breathlessly, "Father's out in the pasture, I think."

"I came to see you," he replied, that great booming voice echoing back from somewhere in the house.

"Oh," I said, looking down at the floor. "Oh, goodness, ah, well, come in."

I backed into a chair, then started to sit down, but suddenly had a picture of the way I must look, flour splattered, my hair coming down from its usual knot. I gulped and ran from the room in a panic. I met Rose on the stairs.

"Who's here?" she asked.

"Mr. Chandler," I squeaked at her, as I slivered past and into my room.

She went on down the stairs and must have invited him

into the parlor, for after I had brushed my hair and changed my dress, that's where I found them, talking away as though they were good friends. I don't think he and I had exchanged a dozen words in my whole life, yet I had promised to marry him. I stood silently a moment in the doorway, trying to gain enough courage to enter.

He looked up and saw me standing there, and my heart seemed to stop beating. Then it began to race so fast and loudly, I was sure they could hear it. I stepped into the room as calmly as I could and took a seat. Rose hadn't blinked or noticed I was there. Mr. Chandler knew though, I could tell. He listened attentively to Rose's ramblings as though the discussion of a girl's clothes was most important. It seemed an hour that she entertained us with her chatter, but it was probably much less time than that. Quietly rising from his chair, his deep voice like thunder rolling in the distance, he excused himself but wondered if Miss McLean would go riding with him. "Of course," Rose, ever vain, jumped to her feet.

"No, Miss Rose, maybe another time. I should like to take your sister, Miss Jewel McLean, riding today." He stood waiting with quiet patience. Rose looked at me with amazement in her eyes, her curiosity no doubt causing the gleam in her eyes.

"Thank you," I said, around the lump in my throat. "I would like to go riding with you. I'll get my shawl."

When I returned, we, as though of one accord, turned toward the kitchen to exit through the back door, and left poor Rose standing alone, her mouth open in surprise, in the middle of the parlor floor.

We walked down the back steps and across to the wagon. He stopped and he smiled, the scar standing out like a white slash across his puckered cheek. A real smile was on his face, and I blinked in shock. I made a move to climb up, but he raised his hands to my waist and gently lifted me up and into the seat. As he went around to the other side, I looked down at my hands clasped tightly in my lap. One of the horses stamped a foot, and I jumped. Me, who had worked with the cattle and with rough, hardened ranch hands, was nervous of this gentle giant. It was a daunting thought.

We rode in his large supply wagon, the one that had made many trips to Virginia and returned full of supplies. My father's wagon was smaller, like a Dearborn, meant for carrying people. I looked around to see if any of the cowboys was watching, half hoping they were, and half mortified that they would see me acting the grand lady. But, no one was in sight. Wait! There was someone. Rose was standing in the back door, her beautiful face puzzled and, I hoped, chagrined. I wanted to stick out my tongue at her. She was so proud of her good looks and slender form. I was sure at that moment that Father hadn't spoken to her of my betrothal.

Picking up the reins, Mr. Chandler started to cluck to the team, but changing his mind, turned to me and gently brushed my cheek with a finger. I looked at him, surprised.

"Flour." Chuckling, he started the horses to moving.

I stared straight ahead at the horses' ears, unable to move or speak. The wagon began to move, and I watched, as though I'd never seen such a thing before, the swaying movement of twin rumps of the large draft horses.

We didn't go far. Over a slight ridge and out of sight of the house and barn, Mr. Chandler stopped the team and applied the brake. We sat in silence. My mind scurried around trying to think of some conversational tidbit, but my tongue and mind wouldn't cooperate.

Mr. Chandler took my slim, cold hand in his massive right hand and covered it with his left.

"Miss McLean," he started to speak at last. Then he stopped, cleared his throat and spoke again.

"Miss McLean." His deep voice rumbled, and my heart fluttered in my chest. "I've received a letter from your father in reply to a proposition that I discussed with him a few weeks back. The letter states that both you and your father are in agreement to the terms of my proposition. I would like to know if you've arrived at your answer of your own free will and determination, without threat on the part of your father. For if you've been coerced in any way, I'll withdraw my offer, and you'll be free to make other plans."

I turned to see that he was gazing at the rumps of the horses just as I had. I couldn't help it. I began to laugh. Laughter bubbled forth, and I sat giggling in the poor man's astonished face. He dropped my hand as though it had turned into a snake in his grasp.

"I'm sorry," I tried to say, my breath coming in gasps. "It was just so funny. The way you and I looked so intently at those horses' rears. I wonder that they don't run away from us in shame."

He looked at the horses, then back at me, puzzled. Finally seeing the joke, he, too, laughed. I saw his eyes sparkle with enjoyment. Then as my gaze lowered to the scar, and then his lips, I sobered and, embarrassed, looked away. He immediately quieted and looked down at his empty hands. He couldn't have known how I wished at that moment that he would kiss me.

I took a deep breath.

"Mr. Chandler," I began. "I've accepted your offer of marriage for two reasons." I could see that he was curious, though he didn't turn to look at me, so I continued.

"Firstly, it was for my father's sake and the future well-being of my family. With your kind offer of financial support, the ranch will become self-supporting and prosperous again. My brother will inherit after my father's death, so his future is secure. My sister will be able to go East to school and, hopefully, find a better life to her liking, for it's as clear as a bell that she hates ranch life."

He turned then and looked at me. I wondered if he thought I was totally mercenary and had proposed to the wrong lady, for my first statements could lead him to just that thought.

"And, your second reason?" There was no expression on his face and he looked back at his hands, waiting patiently. At that moment, dark clouds covered the sun, and I could feel dampness in the air, as though a storm were brewing. One of the horses neighed and stamped his hoof as if in protest. I pulled my shawl closer around my shoulders.

I paused, marshaling my thoughts. "My second reason is an entirely personal one. If I refuse your offer, my father would possibly find another way out of his difficulties, for he's a very determined man, and the ranch is his whole life. I could go east to my aunt, Katherine, in Mississippi where I might chance to meet a man of prominence and wealth and become a great matron of society."

I could feel that he hadn't previously thought that I might ever leave the Territory. He shifted uneasily on the seat but didn't speak. The horses seemed restless and he took the reins to calm them.

"My ambitions have never been that lofty, though." I smiled at the thought. "I hold you in high regard, in spite of my behavior when we first met." The clouds passed and the sun again shone brightly in its splendor in the western sky. I could see by a certain look in his eyes that he was remembering the way I had run from him in fright. "Since then, I have had occasion to witness from a distance your treatment of your customers, your friends and fellow townsmen. You always seem to treat each one with deference and respect, no matter their station or circumstances. Nothing I've ever heard has led me to believe that you wouldn't treat your wife in the same way."

A deep growl of perhaps chagrin or protest rumbled from his throat.

"Miss McLean," he started to speak, but I stopped him with a finger on his lips. His eyes looked at me in silent question. His lips felt moist and soft.

"Besides, I think you're the handsomest man I've ever seen." I blurted out my deepest secret, my face no doubt brick red, for I could feel the warmth of embarrassment on my cheeks and neck.

He sat there stunned. His hand rose to his cheek as though to hide the scar.

"No, don't hide your scar from me. It's not a thing to be ashamed of, but a badge of honor, proudly won on the field of battle for your country. Many men did less and brag of their exploits in the war, yet have nothing visible to prove their courage." I leaned closer and kissed the scar. He backed away and turned his head to the left so I could no longer see his eyes.

"Miss McLean, my dear." The words came out low and somber. "It's only fair to warn you that I have other scars as well. I had thought to remain silent until after the marriage vows, but you've been honest and open with me, and I can do no less."

I think that was the first time I'd heard him speak without his usual authority and pride in his voice. I could feel him trembling and I took his hands in mine.

"Are they bad scars?"

"Yes." He lifted his hand to his left shoulder and spread his fingers out into a wide circle. Pausing a moment, he lowered his hand to his thigh and again circled an area quite large.

"I received two separate wounds, one at Shiloh, where a minny ball pierced my shoulder and left a gaping wound. I lay raging with fever for several days, but the doctors finally were able to patch me up, and I returned to battle. On the day I was captured, I received not only the wound to my face but a sword thrust to the thigh. Without my friend's attention, I would have bled to death. I consider myself very lucky, for so many of my comrades died without assistance." He didn't move and spoke softly and calmly.

"And your friend, what happened to him?" I asked.

"He died," he replied bluntly, no emotion in his voice. I could sense that he had grieved deeply for his friend, but now had put his grief behind him, just as he had the betrayal of his fiancée. I didn't press him for more. I placed my hand over his, still lying on his thigh, where the wound had almost cost him his life.

He took my hand, raised it to his lips, and placing a gentle kiss on the outside, turned it over and placed another kiss in the palm. Solemnly and with dignity, he asked, "Miss McLean, will you do me the great honor of becoming my wife?"

"Mr. Chandler, I will marry you," I replied quietly, more certain than ever that it was the right answer. He drew me into his arms and sealed the promise with his lips on mine. It was my first kiss, and I'm not sure what I expected. His lips were warm and soft and sweet. He pulled me tighter, and I could sense passion and ardor, yet he restrained his emotions. His arms were strong, yet gentle, and I could feel the texture of his suit coat as I lifted my arms to his shoulders and smelled the faint scent of spice and tobacco. He drew back and looked at me. I reached up and caressed his scarred face. He smiled and kissed me again. As soft as a butterfly's wings, the touch seemed not at all as the first one had.

"Thank you," he said, humbly, as though it was a truly great honor for him. "Now, I think I'd better return you to your sister before she begins to think that I've kidnapped you." He paused. "Miss McLean, I would appreciate your silence on the matter of my wounds, just as I will never reveal to anyone the circumstances of our marriage."

"You have my word. I'll never speak of the discussion we've had today without your consent." I smiled, but his countenance remained grave. He turned and picked up the reins. The wagon began to move in the direction of the ranch house.

For a few moments, we were both silent, lost in our thoughts. As though our earlier discussion had never taken place, he began to talk of our marriage day. "I think the preacher will be in town in two weeks, if he holds true to his monthly schedule. Will that be too soon for you to get ready?"

Surprised but not dismayed, I replied, "That'll give me plenty of time. I don't need a lot of preparations. It's not my style."

"We'll live behind the store, of course, for now. You can make any changes in the living quarters that you wish. I have plans to build a house in the future, maybe after my next trip to Virginia. I'll bring back lumber and furniture with me from the East. I've already purchased some town lots. We should be in our new home within a year, maybe two." He continued talking about the house, and I could see that he'd spent a great deal of time thinking about it. A twinge of anxiety passed through me as I remembered that he'd possibly made similar plans for his fickle lover in Virginia. Or, maybe he had someone else in mind, but because he felt sorry for my father's situation had decided that I'd do as well. No, I was being foolish. I chastised myself, for he wouldn't have offered for me in that case. He was an honorable man. He wouldn't have left a girl dangling in Virginia, for he'd learned that lesson well. I thought what might happen if I too withdrew from our agreement.

The afternoon shadows were lengthening across the

prairie, and I shivered. The clouds were becoming fierce and angry.

"I must get you back. The wind's shifted, and it's becoming cooler."

At the house, he lifted me from my high perch on the wagon seat and walked with me to the door.

"I may not have time to come this way before the wedding. I'll be busy with the store. If you have need of me, send word by one of the cowboys, and I'll come to you."

"Thank you," I replied. "I'm sure everything will be fine."

"Goodbye, Miss McLean." He turned away from me as though our conversation had been a casual one with a customer in his store. I was mortified after my forward behavior during the afternoon.

"Goodbye, Mr. Chandler."

From the shelter of the window screen, I watched as he climbed aboard the wagon and drove out of sight over the ridge, heading toward town.

Rose came clambering down the stairs, clearly curious and watching for my return. Her cheeks were rosy, and her forehead moist from her haste. She stopped a few feet away and stared.

"You're back." She greeted me as though that fact was not perfectly obvious. "What was Mr. Chandler doing here? Where did you go with him?" Her eyes had a greedy gleam, and I could tell that she was jealous.

"We're to be married. He was extending a formal proposal to me and wanted some privacy, I suppose." I casually threw my shawl onto the sofa.

Rose squealed and rung her hands until her fingers became white and her nails bit into the skin. I watched in fascination the display of emotion from a girl who'd never seemed to care about my affairs before today.

"Married? You're going to marry Mr. Chandler and

you didn't tell me?"

"I just told you. Father arranged it, but Mr. Chandler wanted to ask me himself, in privacy." I couldn't prevent the little sly dig at her vanity.

"I shan't let Father arrange my marriage," she exclaimed with a defiant toss of her blonde curls. "I shall choose for myself, and he won't be an ugly shopkeeper. My husband will be rich or maybe a politician, and we'll live in Washington City or Philadelphia.' Her eyes took on that envious glow that I'd seen many times before. "Maybe I'll marry a banker and live in New York. I'd love to live in New York and have fancy dresses and go to balls. I certainly don't intend to spend my life in this dead place."

She followed me into the kitchen, still exclaiming about her future, but I didn't mind, because for the first time since our mother had died, Rose seemed animated and interested in something beside her hair or the color of her dress. I silently thanked Mr. Chandler for that blessing.

I spent a week making my dress for the wedding. I used careful, small stitches as my mother had taught me. Father had purchased the material as a surprise some time back for my eighteenth birthday, but I hadn't gotten around to using it. I felt my mother's presence with every stitch.

Rose continued in a cheerful yet resentful mood. She pleaded for a new dress of her own, but I explained that there wasn't enough time to sew another. I refurbished one of her old ones by adding some lace and a ruffle around the bottom. I wondered often during that time how Father and my brother would manage after I left the house. Rose had been taught to cook just as I had, but she was only sixteen. I thought probably Old Pete, the bunkhouse cook, would prepare their meals, if necessary. It was time and enough for Rose to assume some of the household chores as I had done when our mother died.

I knew that Father received the money from Mr.

Chandler, because several of the hands were sent to Abilene to purchase cattle and a bull. He wanted to go himself but sent Thomas instead as his representative. It was a great adventure for my brother. He'd never been more than a few miles from home, for all his twenty years of age. To go with the hands without Father to supervise his actions, I'm sure made him feel independent and grown-up. I only hoped he wouldn't get into some mischief, for the cowboys themselves were sometimes wild when on a cattle drive.

On the day before our marriage, I took some wild daisies and laid them on my mother's grave behind the white fence on the hill. I knelt on the damp grass and placed my hands together in prayer.

"Mother, I don't know if you would approve of my marrying Mr. Chandler. He wasn't a stranger to you, for you'd known him very well; and liked him, I think. He'll suit me fine, for I don't expect any great political or social life as Rose does. I do so want to go to Virginia someday. Maybe he'll take me to buy supplies next year. I'll be able to see the tall trees and the large plantations, even if they're different from your own home in Mississippi. Darling Mother, bless my marriage tomorrow if you can. I want to be as happy as you were in my own home and with my children. I want to be a good and true wife to Mr. Chandler and make him comfortable."

Feeling a little foolish for talking to a stone, I turned away and returned to the house.

*****

I awoke early on my wedding day and was appalled to realize that it was raining. Still, I heated water and bathed and washed my hair. I sat in front of the cook stove while drying it and finished the last stitches to Rose's dress. I brushed my thick hair and lamented the dull brown color, as I had many times in the past. Why had I not been graced with shining blonde hair like my sister? Or even the pale locks of my mother before it became streaked with gray? After it was dry, I piled it on top of my head with pins and covered it with a cloth as protection while I cooked breakfast. I began to regret my early bath, because the smell of biscuits and fried bacon permeated the room. After breakfast, I washed up and went to dress. I found a small bottle partly filled with perfume in a drawer and thought that might help drive away the smell of bacon, but it smelled worse than the bacon, so I left it in the drawer, unused.

By ten o'clock, we were on our way, Father, Rose and me. Thomas was still on the trip to Abilene so didn't attend my wedding. I wrapped an old wool coat of Father's around me to keep the damp from spoiling my dress. Rose wore one of Old Pete's coats. We were a sorry sight, two girls with wilted hats and smelly, damp wool coats. Father's suit became soaked.

Just as we arrived at Mrs. Alice Jennings' door, the sun came out, leaving the horse steaming. The yard was full of people, mostly men, for they outnumbered the women in the Territory. Mrs. Jennings greeted us happily and drew us into the room. Caroline and Evelyn, her twin daughters, swooped on us, exclaiming over our flattened hair and damp dresses, in spite of our efforts to protect them from the wet. Rose's hair, as usual, sprang into tiny curls around her face, making her very pretty. Mine lay flat. Mrs. Jennings clucked like a hen.

"Oh, you poor child, and on your wedding day, too," she said. She and Caroline brushed and pinned, but there was no hope. It remained flat. I finally laughed and told them to desist. What couldn't be changed had to be endured.

The parlor was transformed into a flower garden.

Thankfully, the girls had picked the flowers the day before. Arranged in three vases, June roses sat on a table in one corner, beside Mrs. Jennings' favorite chair and over the mantle. A wide table covered by a soft linen cloth was placed in the middle of the room, and on it sat a large bowl filled with apple cider, and an iced raisin cake, sinfully sweet. There were two other brides that day, strangers from ranches miles away. To this very day, I can't remember their names, in spite of sharing the same wedding celebration. Since the preacher came only once a month to our small town, all marriages and baptisms were performed on the same day. The girls' mothers were making last minute preparations for the ceremony. At last, they were satisfied that everything was perfect, and the men were invited in.

The room didn't hold everyone, of course, so the principle players in the drama were arranged on one side of the room, with the three brides standing next to their grooms, the parents on the outskirts, with the preacher standing in front of the punch bowl table. The few women were allowed to sit in the chairs present, with the men standing in the doorways.

I heard a gasp of shock when Mr. Chandler took his place beside me, straight and tall. He took my hand in his, and I felt cherished and safe in his care. I could smell his spicy hair tonic and wondered if he smelled the bacon on me. I almost giggled out loud at the thought. His vows were pronounced in his deep, booming voice, mine in a nervous squeak of sound. Some of the strangers glanced at him from time to time, as though his scarred face made them uneasy. But, to the townspeople and his customers, he was familiar, and no one in the town was more respected, I believe.

The ceremony itself was short, but the social time afterward stretched long into the afternoon. Rose received a good deal of attention from the men. Her beauty far outshone any other girl in the room, even the brides in their finery. She didn't flirt, exactly, just smiled and laughed and talked. At sixteen, she was far too young to know about flirting, but the men swarmed around her like bees. Mrs. Jennings had the only piano in town, and she played for hours, while everyone danced, whirling around in circles so small, it was hard not to bump into your partner or another couple. To my great surprise, Mr. Chandler took my hand and drew me into the center of the room. We danced and danced. He would allow no one else to dance with me, saying that I was his bride. I wanted to be angry, but I was overwhelmed by the feelings inside me. Butterflies as big as my horse, Nellie, fluttered in my stomach. The smell of sweat, wilted flowers and stale perfume made me nauseous.

Finally, sensing my discomfort, Mr. Chandler took me aside.

"Are you ready to go?" There was a somber gleam in his eyes, as he gazed at me with something like compassion.

I nodded my head, tears gathering in my eyes. We said a quick goodbye to Father and Rose, thanked Mrs. Jennings politely, and left.

It had rained again during the celebration, but had since stopped. The sky was dark gray, and the grass sparkled like tiny pieces of glass. Mr. Chandler handed me into the wagon, and I thought we would go but a short distance to the store, but he kept on driving west until the town was out of sight. A prankster had tied ribbons and old cans filled with pebbles behind the wagon, but Mr. Chandler left them there, the ribbons flying in the breeze, and the cans bouncing and rattling. On and on we went, farther than I had ever been in that direction. Off in the distance, I saw a clump of trees. I looked at my new husband, questioningly. He laughed.

"I thought we would get away from town until some of the rowdier men become discouraged and go back to their ranches."

"Why? I don't understand."

"Haven't you ever been to a wedding before?" His hands were steady on the reins, and the horses clop, clopped as though to music.

I shook my head no.

"Never heard of a chivaree?"

Again I shook my head.

"I'll explain when we stop."

I decided I'd simply enjoy the ride so stopped asking question. He seemed relieved and clucked to the horses. They walked slowly but steadily west. They weren't what you would call pretty horses, like the wild mustangs my father used on the range, just draft horses, used for pulling heavy loads. I could now make out a winding river with trees on each side, not large trees, but small willows and pin oaks. Mr. Chandler pulled the reins, and the horses turned toward the trees. He stopped beside a drooping willow. Its branches hung nearly to the ground, heavy from the rain on its leaves. I heard the tinkling sound of the brook as it wandered downhill. I sighed.

"This is a pretty spot," I said. "It's so different from the plains."

"Yes, very pretty," he replied, looking at me. I could feel a flutter in my breast.

"Do you like it?"

"Very much."

"I discovered it on the day I first came to this area. I bought three acres when it came up for sale. If you like it, this is where we'll make our home."

"But, isn't it too far from town?"

"I figure someday, the town will be out here."

I stared at him in amazement. The town would grow so big that it would reach out to this pretty river? My mind couldn't grasp the concept. I looked around me, then back at my husband.

"Yes." He pulled me into his arms and kissed me gently, first on the forehead, then the nose, then the chin and at last, on the lips. I could feel the wonder of the moment and knew that he was saying something important, but my senses were overwhelmed by the glory of being held in his arms. "Someday the town will reach far beyond the current boundaries. And, we'll grow with it. The store and our children will fill our lives with satisfaction, and someday, our grandchildren will play tag along this riverbank."

I blushed. I knew he expected children; all men did. But, I'd put it to the back of my mind in my excitement. He helped me down from the wagon, tied the horses' reins to a tree, and reached into the back of the wagon for some quilts. He set up a small army tent on the spot, and we spent the first night of marriage under the old willow that now stretches its boughs over the flower garden and can be seen from my kitchen window. I cooked our supper over an open fire, and we gazed at the sky trying to count the stars. It was a lovely night after the rain of the morning.

— 4 —

We were married less than a year when Father came to the store one day to talk to Mr. Chandler. They sat in the makeshift office, a nook near the bedroom door leading to the kitchen area, and whispered among themselves for a long time, while I sat and knitted tiny sweaters for the babies of the town. I decided they might sell in the store, and it gave me something to do with my hands at night, while my husband toted up the figures for the day. Father kissed me goodbye with a satisfied look on his countenance, and I knew that the conversation had gone his way. Although I pressed him for answers, my husband wouldn't come forth until the next day, when the telegraph agent brought him an urgent note.

It seemed that my sister Rose had gotten out of hand, and Father decided to accompany her east to live with our aunt Katherine in Mississippi. Mr. Chandler paid their fare and gave her some spending money for her pocket. On a Saturday morning in late August, they boarded the train for the eastern United States. We all turned out for her departure; the shopkeepers and the cowhands, Mr. Chandler and some of the townspeople who knew us well, and me in my new Sunday-go-to-meeting dress of a dark pink rose color. I wore a new straw hat that came in the batch from St. Louis decorated with pink feathers and a wide black band. I had become quite popular for my hat decorations by that time. They come by the dozen in a large round box from St. Louis. And, a separate selection of feathers, ribbons and wax flowers could be bought for a penny a pound. But, I get ahead of my tale.

Rose looked lovely standing on the platform, all in light blue to match her eyes. She always liked girly things, and her dress had white eyelet lace with tiny blue ribbon threaded through it on the arms, neck, and waist. She had grown proficient in sewing her own garments by the time she was seventeen. I was proud of her, standing there that day. The conductor waved to the engineer, and she boarded the train with Father who was dressed in his best overalls and shoes. He had a bowler hat on his head, and he looked so tired before the journey even started. My last sight of them was the white handkerchief she hung out the window in farewell.

Father returned a week later and told us about the trip and the sights and sounds of Mississippi. Oh, how I longed to go east in those days. Aunt Katherine was well, and our cousins married with children. It was just as Mother had described in her stories of her childhood, and I knew that Rose would be happy there. We didn't hear from her for the longest time, but we got a letter from Aunt Katherine. She enrolled Rose in a fancy school for young girls where she would learn comportment, dancing, sewing, languages, and other things too numerous to mention. She chose French, and I could imagine my Rose swooning in the French way onto a chaise, while the other girls laughed with her. She was destined for the stage, but Father was so straight-laced he would never have allowed it.

I got a letter before Christmas from Rose, and she told

of the huge magnolia trees, the dark summer nights with the fireflies dancing in the air, and the cottonwoods covering the fields like snow, but she never mentioned the beaus or the parties without herself as the heroine. She graduated from Mrs. Lucille Treackle's Academy for Girls in the spring of the following year with a certificate of merit in French and Mathematics. How proud of her, I was. Mr. Chandler thought she would come back to the Territory, but Father received a letter from Aunt Katherine about her marriage in July to Mr. John Beldon of Philadelphia.

It was a grand affair, with over a hundred people attending, she said. It was held in the Roman Catholic Cathedral, for Mr. John Beldon was Somebody in politics. I remembered the way Rose would swoon and carry on in her prissy way as a child, and I was happy that she'd gotten what she wanted. She wore a white satin and lace dress and carried white roses with pale blue ribbons in her hand, and real satin slippers. They went on a trip to Niagara Falls in New York and settled down in Philadelphia where Mr. Beldon had his law office. She wrote me a month later, and I could tell that she was pleased with her new life. How our aunt Katherine and Father, of course, missed her, but I had enough to keep me busy without worrying about my sister.

There was a County Fair that spring, and the town was filled with strangers who'd come into the Territory to see the sights. There was a bearded lady, and a fat lady, a midget, and a man who could swallow fire. There was also a man who walked on stilts. Oh, it was exciting, and I gazed in wonder at the sights and ate salted peanuts from a small bag. Later, after the turn of the Century, there were the Circuit Chatauquas, but I'll never forget that first County Fair in the Territory.

The store was a popular spot in those days for the residents of the town, and we were busy every day. Mr.

Pollard and his cronies would sit and tell stories about their days in the war. Mr. Chandler never said a word about his own wounds while the men were talking. But, later when we were alone, he told me how silly the men were, bragging about their exploits.

"They seem to have forgotten the cruelties of war, the sight of the dead and injured men on the ground, the smell of gun powder and the buzzards flying in the sky," he told me.

He would shake his head and take a turn about the town to clear his head, and return without the scornful frown on his face. Eventually, the men ceased talking of the war as their memories began to fade and their companions grew older or moved away.

Leopold Pollard was an odd little man, who spoke with a heavy accent. He was barely five feet tall and stout of build. He grew a long, gray beard and was bald on top. The men teased him about that, to have hair on his face, but not his head. He wore an old beaver top hat to keep the sun from his head. He had come to America when a youth from Poland, to work in a tailor shop in New York City. He told us of the tall buildings and the smells along the riverfront where he would go to spend his free afternoons. There were stalls where the merchants sold different kinds of fish that came on the ships off shore, and vegetables and fruits. The children would play stick ball in the streets, and the women hung their clothing on a cord out of their high windows. He made fine suits for the men and boys. I could see him hunched over his stitching with the light growing dim as I walked past the window of his shop. One day he received a letter from his nephew in Poland that he was coming to New York, and Mr. Pollard decided to move back to the city. It was on the same day that a customer's rowdy boys knocked over a barrel of potatoes, and we spent the afternoon chasing after them under the counters and behind the stove. It must have been a funny sight, us on our hands and knees searching for the potatoes.

There were sad times, too. It was shortly after Mr. Pollard stepped into the store for the last time to say goodbye that the influenza epidemic held the town in its grasp for weeks. Little children died, and old folks gave up the ghost without a whimper. We had to close the store because everyone was afraid to venture out of their houses. Some nights, a man would knock on the back door and ask for something he needed, but mostly we watched the sickness from the front windows. The droll funeral cortege would drive down the street to the graveyard, the newspaper dutifully wrote the names, and kinsfolk would mourn the passing of another soul. Mr. Chandler kept a secret list of names of families who had to buy their staples on credit, for the times were bad, and with the sickness, the men couldn't work. Dr. Griffith, the old doctor, was kept busy, and he wrote for a younger man, a Dr. Smith, an Army doctor from Fort Sill, to come help him.

Dr. Smith was a very handsome man, tall and gangly with a winning smile, and Mr. Chandler teased me about him, for he came into the store often for some little item that he would purchase for his patients to cheer them up, especially the peppermint stick candy and the red cherry drops. We ran out of them before the epidemic was over and had only the licorice left to give the children. The whistles, pen knives and coloring books disappeared into Dr. Smith's pockets to be distributed among the little ones in his care. I never knew his first name, for as soon as the sickness left the town, Dr. Smith drove back to Fort Sill and his Army responsibilities.

During the epidemic, Mr. Chandler decided that since business was slacked off, it was a good time to hold an inventory of the items in the store. He got a sheet of brown meat-wrapping paper, and I carefully wrote down the items, how many and what kind, the price at wholesale and at retail, and whether we had sold any of them lately, for sometimes things would sit on the shelves for months, unwanted. I kept a separate list of things to order when he next went to Virginia for supplies. The dust moved around the store like a fog as we shifted, stacked, separated and dusted the items. I'm not sure we accomplished anything at all, but Mr. Chandler was pleased, and so, I was, too. After that day, we did an inventory once each year, on New Year's Day while the other people were celebrating the passing of the old year. He said it was better to keep a regular schedule. We'd know how we'd progressed through the year and could toss out or give away the things that hadn't sold. Mr. Chandler was a wise man.

I can see him now, high on the ladder, reaching for that last can of soup or that last tin cup or lantern on the shelf, the scar on his face visible through the sweat as he strained and groaned. After living with my man for some years, I hardly noticed the scars on his face and body, but sometimes he would ask me to rub grease or a salve on them, for they ached or drew tight and dry in the hot sun or the strain of muscles. A few times, he called out in the night, the name of some fellow who had died beside him in battle, but when he awoke, he couldn't remember the dream, or he told me he couldn't, so as not to worry me.

Most days, he was cheerful and told some simple story that amused the men sitting around the pot-bellied stove during the winter. It was a popular gathering spot on long, snowy days when the farmers and merchants couldn't work. They'd play games of chance or sit, smoking their pipes or cigars, and telling of the days of yore before they moved to the Territory, each one trying to outdo the other one. I'd listen for a while and go into the living quarters to make tea or coffee or hot soup for the men. I'd make corn pones with the soup, or muffins or cookies to eat with their drinks. Mr. Chandler said at least it kept them out of the saloons.

Father came to the store more often after Rose moved east. He seemed lonely and tired. I worried about him working so hard, and said that Thomas should take on more responsibility, but he said that it was his farm, and Thomas had his own life to see about. My brother married my friend Evelyn Jennings, the twin daughter of Alice Jennings, the war widow.

Caroline, Evelyn and I had some gay times together. They were a few years older than I, but the most nearly of my age in the one room log schoolhouse. We would brush each other's hair, braid it, and giggle over some silly joke that only we knew. We learned to dance together and had tea parties with soda crackers and real tea, provided by their mother. Alice put milk in her tea, and Caroline learned to drink it that way, but Evelyn and I liked ours plain with a cube of sugar and some lemon, if they were available. They were very rare and came from California. Sometimes, a peddler would bring some up from Texas, but we didn't have lemons as a regular treat.

The year before his marriage, Thomas was in a card game in the Red Slipper Saloon on the edge of town and was accused by one of the men of cheating. It ended in a gun fight, and Brother was injured in the shoulder. Dr. Griffith sobered up long enough to take the bullet out, but he caught a fever and almost died. Father sat with him for long hours, and Mr. Chandler and I stayed at night in the little back room that served in those days as a hospital. My brother lay so pale and wan in that large walnut bed that had been in Dr. Griffith's family for years before the war. I dipped the cloth in cool water and bathed him all over several times a night to bring the fever down. He moaned and yelled out some curse words that even I, who grew up among the cowboys, hadn't heard before. Finally, he came out of it and was better. I made him homemade soup, with a little beef and potatoes to give him strength, and chicken broth for sustenance.

Old Mack Webster gave me a couple of chickens, and Mr. Chandler rung their necks and dressed them for me. We didn't have any animals in the town, wouldn't have had time to care for them if we did. Mr. Chandler offered to pay for the chickens, but Mr. Webster wouldn't have it. He said he felt like Thomas got a raw deal, being shot for something he didn't do, for the sheriff investigated the card game, and it was found that a stranger named Bellows was the one who had cheated and shot Thomas to cover it up. He went to trial and got a few months in jail. As soon as he was released, he caught the train out of town. It was best so, for if my brother had gotten hold of him, there'd have been more shooting. Mr. Webster was in on the card game that night and saw the whole thing, so he said the least he could do was give us the chickens to feed Brother.

There was a great wave of moral indignation that swept through the town during the investigation. A fallen woman named Berthena Evans had opened a place near the saloon on the outskirts of town that she called a gentlemen's retreat. One night, a group of women marched to the place with torches and told Madam Evans that it would be best if she and her friends left town, or she might regret it. Mr. Chandler and I had worked late at the store, trying to pick up the pieces from a box of broken liver tonic bottles that had arrived damaged. We heard the noise, saw the movement of the torches through the front windows and rushed to the front door to see the end of the commotion. One of the "gentlemen" was being led by the ear from the house, by his very angry wife. We could hardly control our laughter as he was marched down the street to the sound of loud taunts and shouts. The house stayed vacant for years, as no one wanted to live in a place with such a reputation. It was finally torn down. Years later, a new building was raised there, and it became a fire station. I laugh as I write the words, to think that a fire station replaced the house that a group of righteous women threatened to burn down.

— 5 —

Thomas and Evelyn started their married life in the old farm house where I grew up, but increasingly, he and Father argued over which crops to grow or whether to sell the cattle in the spring or something, and Thomas bought the lumber and built his own house. Their five children were born in the new house. They named the eldest Thomas Junior. He's a good man, made high marks in his school days, and won the spelling bee every year. The teacher, Janice Yancy, asked him not to participate one year, so the others would have a chance at the prize, which was usually a book or a box of water colors.

With Thomas moved out, Father was left alone in the large house with no one but the housekeeper, Mrs. Pettigrew, to care for his needs. She was a kind lady and a good cook. We went to the ranch a few times when business was slow to have a family gettogether. She made a kind of raisin and pecan cake with an egg white frosting that was delicious. I got the recipe from her, but it never tasted the same when I baked it. She loved strawberries, and Father dug a small plot for her. They were so sweet and juicy; I could have eaten her strawberries by the pound. She made jam with them and brought us a few jars every year. After a few years, Mrs. Pettigrew moved to Chicago to live with her sister. She had the lumbago something awful and was no longer able to do for Father as she wanted.

We interviewed a couple of women, but they didn't seem to be good housekeepers. Alice Jennings told us about a widow lady in Greer County who needed work to support herself. Mr. Chandler and I drove the wagon over to the county and talked to her. She fixed a meal for us, and although it wasn't as good as Mrs. Pettigrew's, it was sufficient for Father's needs, so she agreed to come to us. She stayed a week, and we got to know her well. Father approved of her, and she moved into the big house. She had several grown children and a few grandchildren, and they livened up Father's days when they came to visit. The children would ride the horses and the young bulls and learned to rope and brand the cattle. I envied them their youth and enthusiasm.

Neva Fitzsimmons was her name, and she was in her late 40's when she went to work for Father at the ranch. She was there when he died, and we all loved her and her children and grandchildren. She was like an older sister to me. We spent long hours talking about food and canning and gardening and female things. I had a second family group for those years. I caught her once flirting with Mr. Chandler and told him he better behave, or I'd scratch her eyes out, and they never caused me more trouble. He said it was in good fun, for all he was old enough to be her brother, and I loved them both well.

More and more Thomas took over the operation of the ranch, the hiring and firing and supervising the hired hands and the buying and selling. It was frustrating for my father to watch his son take over, but his health was fragile after my mother's death and the awful drought year when I was married to Mr. Chandler. He came to us many days and helped a bit in the store. He seemed to enjoy the company of the other merchants and farmers who sat around the pot-bellied stove. When Mr. Chandler got the contract for the United States Mail for the District, Father would sort the mail for him when he was in town. At first he rode his stallion, Juniper, to town, but later he would come in the wagon, with the excuse of buying supplies for the ranch, and Mr. Chandler would send him home with something to back up the excuse, but really he came for companionship, I think. Mr. Chandler would talk to him as though they were brothers, and since Father had left his family behind in Mississippi, it served him well to have someone of his age and generation to talk with.

Another incident happened in those early years of our marriage that seems important enough to disclose. The wagon train from Virginia was about forty miles from our town when a band of painted Indians attacked it, about a dozen men, yelling and shooting into the air. They seemed to know what was in the wagons, for they only took the food supplies and boxes of clothes, shoes and medicines. Caesar Mangard, our loyal driver, received a broken arm when his wagon turned over onto its side, but the settlers weren't disturbed. A few courageous men fired weapons but weren't harmed. The train consisted of the two large Chandler freight wagons and six settlers' wagons, a dozen men on horseback, and some one hundred or so loose cattle, horses and mules. They drove off the cattle and horses and left some of the people to walk the rest of the way. It was a bad situation for us, for we were left short of supplies for the coming winter months.

One of the settlers rode to Fort Sill and reported the incident to the authorities, but we never heard whether the men were caught and punished. Mr. Chandler and Caesar went to Fort Sill, but there was little to be bought there. We were able to buy some wheat from a farmer, and it was ground into flour at Mason's mill, but it was a hard season for the whole town. The farmers helped their neighbors as best they could with vegetables from their gardens, eggs and corn, and Father contributed five cows for meat. The other ranchers pitched in with hay and grain, and a couple of hunters tagged some deer for the townspeople. Caesar started back East before the frost left the ground to bring back more supplies. He and Mr. Chandler decided that Virginia was too far, so he went only as far as Fort Smith in Arkansas that year.

It was during the fire of 1886 that I lost my horse, Nellie. I was in the store waiting on Mrs. Samantha White, who lived at the south end of town and didn't come into the store often. I think they were very poor. I smelled smoke and rushed into the living quarters, thinking I might have left a pot on the stove, and she followed me. We found no fire or smoke. We moved into the store and watched through the front window as people began to gather in the street. I closed the door and went outside. There on the horizon on the north was a large black smoke cloud. Mr. Chandler had taken the deposit to the bank, and I saw him as he came out, puzzled at the number of people, and saw the smoke. He ran to my side, for we both knew that my father's ranch was in that direction. He told me he would go see what was happening. He saddled the horse and rode away.

Other men were riding and driving buggies and wagons, all headed toward the smoke. The women gathered in the street, watching and waiting. Some of the shopkeepers stayed behind to guard their shops in case the fire came toward town. Caroline wandered over to the bank to be with her husband and her mother. They knew that Evelyn was at the ranch with Thomas and Father. Samantha went home to her family, and I went back to the store, praying for my family on the ranch. It lasted for hours, and some stragglers came into town with the news.

The fire was very large. It covered hundreds of acres and destroyed not only my father's ranch, but our neighbors on the north and east. Father, Thomas and the hands were successful in saving the house, but the barn and corrals were gone. My horse, Nellie, was burned in her stall, and Smokey, one of the greatest range horses in the land, was killed; also, our old milk cow, Lila, and a dozen or more chickens, but not the hogs, because they were in the mud wallow. One of the cowhands, an older gentleman named Oscar, whom I had many times ridden the range with, was caught in a gulley and unable to breathe for the smoke. They found his body where he lay; his horse beside him. Mr. Chandler rode home late in the dark night with the sad news.

Sweet Evelyn was burned on her arms and hands, and her eyebrows singed trying to save her baby. She ran until she was exhausted and dived into the cattle pond, holding the baby high to keep him from drowning. She was the real heroine of the day, for she didn't know what she left behind her, her husband, father-in-law and the hands. She instinctively thought of the future of the ranch, and to save the baby was her cry for mercy. She was unable to care for the child for weeks, and Neva cared for him. She hadn't been at the ranch that day, thankfully. She was visiting one of her children. She was able to care for Evelyn and the baby, and tend to the wounds of the cowhands.

Father and Thomas had minor wounds, and one of the hands was taken to Fort Sill to the Army hospital, but he miraculously survived. Mr. Chandler closed the store the next day, and we drove to see my family. We did what we could, brought food staples, blankets and fresh water in buckets; salves and medicines from the doctor; and canned milk for the children. I stayed at the ranch for a week, while Mr. Chandler worked in the store. The town was quiet as though the whole community mourned. We buried Oscar in our family plot near my mother and brother. He had been a loyal employee and had no family that we knew about. Caroline and her mother came to help Evelyn. Alice stayed until long after I left, but Caroline went home to care for her own family.

The lovely green pastures of the morning were now black and parched, still smoking in spots, and dead cattle were lying for miles on the ground. All the cattlemen had to bunch their brands together in one field to hold the remnants of the herds together. They bought hay from the ranchers and farmers in the south, who kept the prices low to help their neighbors. Some of the ranchers were able to get personal loans from the bank, and eventually, the government helped with the cost of grain and barn building, but it was a long few years before the community was again prosperous.

Mr. Chandler gave Father enough money to build another barn. This time he didn't ask for a daughter as collateral, for Father had no more daughters. Thomas had saved enough to buy a new bull, but the rest had to wait until spring when they could have a round-up and sell off some cattle to make the payroll and fix the fences and corrals. Thomas received in the mail a cashier's check on the bank from Rose's husband, John Beldon, to make repairs on the house or pay for medical bills for the hands. We were grateful for the gesture of love and support.

One of my best friends in the town during that time was named Janice Yancy. I always thought that was a funny name, Yancy. She and her parents and siblings came to town about five years after Mr. Chandler and I were married. She was kind and thoughtful, always cheerful, and made a wonderful mother to their five children. She was the school teacher for several years until she married Sam Raymond, the new Methodist preacher.

Christopher and Maud Yancy were from New Orleans, but they originally came from somewhere north, I think. Janice never said. They lived in New Orleans while she was growing up and couldn't remember where they lived before she was born. They had a house full of children, of which Janice was the oldest. I seem to remember a Ronnie, a Jimmie and a Mable, but there were so many children who came into the store through the years, I can't remember all their names. The parents stayed and farmed for about six or seven years after her marriage and later moved to St. Louis or somewhere in Missouri. Janice would know, since she stayed behind and married Sam Raymond.

We had an itinerant preacher who visited once a month and moved on to the other communities in the Territory. All the weddings, funeral services, baptisms and child christenings were held while he was here. He usually stayed a day or two, sometimes a week if someone would feed and house him for that length of time, but I think he made most people in the household uncomfortable, being so religious and all. The first one I remember was Reverend Lavender, a Southern gentleman of the first order, snow white beard and hair. I always thought of him as Moses, who led the Israelites out of the wilderness. His wife was short and stout and had a lovely smile, as though she were an angel. She could dry a child's tears or scold her for some non-important mischief with equal ability. I loved her. Next, there was Reverend Malachi Kennedy, who was the parson who married Mr. Chandler and me, and the other two couples who shared our wedding day.

Reverend Kennedy was not as sweet or gentle as Mr. Lavender, but a good man, all the same. He was more somber, in his white collar, black suit and shiny shoes. I asked Mr. Chandler after we were wed how he kept his shoes so clean, and my husband said he used beer to polish them. I gaped in surprise. A preacher who used beer to polish his shoes? I think Mr. Chandler was teasing me, but I knew nothing of a man's toiletries, so pretended to believe him. Mr. Kennedy preached long sermons about hell and damnation, fire and brimstone, and ashes and clothes of scarlet. I was half frightened when he spoke, and was glad that I was married and not tempted to stray from the Good Shepherd's flock.

He led the congregation in songs and didn't frown on dancing or musical instruments, as some preachers did, saying that they used them in King David's time, so why should we judge the modern folks? It was traditional in the Bible. He had a lovely tenor voice and often sang a solo for the people. Mr. Chandler sang in his deep, masculine bass, and it thrilled me to hear him. Mr. Chandler and I loved to dance and didn't have many opportunities, so took advantage when the preacher came to visit. We would've liked to have had him to stay in our home, but at that time, we lived in the two rooms behind the store. He ate many of his meals with us when he was in the area. Mr. Kennedy and Mr. Chandler liked to sit and talk of politics or religion, or other interesting, exotic things, like Pharaoh's palace, or the Jewish Temple Guards, and I would sit with my knitting in my hands and listen, as quiet as a church mouse. Oh, that's funny, for we had no church building then.

It was after Mr. Kennedy took a permanent position in a church in Louisiana that we built the first church building. Mr. Kennedy told Mr. Chandler that it was a temptation he wasn't strong enough to resist, to have his own congregation, and to stop the endless travel, for by that time, he was married and had a growing family. It was usually the single pastors who took the traveling assignments, I think. We missed Mr. Kennedy, for he was a special man, for all his talk of hell and damnation in his sermons. It was so contradictory to his love of music and dancing. His wife's name was Susie, and she was a replica of Mrs.

Lavender, only younger. She held my hand and prayed with me on the night my only child was stillborn. It was a terrible night of pain and sorrow and fear.

Mr. Chandler and I had so looked forward to the birth of our first child, but it wasn't to be. I knitted sweaters and booties, and made dozens of tiny dresses with lace and a special dress for the christening service. I was certain it would be a girl, but Mr. Chandler teased me and began to choose boy names. I was in my seventh month when the pains came, excruciating and long, until I screamed with the agony. Mr. Chandler left me for only the time to go after Alice Jennings to assist me until Dr. Griffith came. It seemed there was a multitude of people in the house that day. It was the time for Mr. Kennedy's visit, and he and Susie came and prayed with us. She was alone with me when the babe was born. I heard no cry or whimper of sound and fainted.

When I awoke, I was alone with Mr. Chandler, and his eyes were bleak and red from weeping. He told me gently of the stillborn boy that he had held in his arms for only a moment before the doctor took him away. He named him Amos Rudolph Chandler, after himself and his father. He buried him in the christening dress of white. They had a small service in the home of Alice Jennings for my baby, without me, for I was too ill to attend. When I think back on the day, I feel blessed that Mr. Kennedy was there to christen him and say the words of grace over my son.

I was in bed for a week, then arose and returned to my duties as wife and shopkeeper. We talked of the future, of more children, but I was barren. It wasn't until years later that we accepted the fact, took pleasure in our nieces and nephews, and felt blessed for having them to balance our life's journey. I was never one for visiting graveyards, but I carried flowers to the grave of my son every year on his birthday, until Mr. Chandler was laid beside him, and I stopped the romantic gesture, for Amos has his father to comfort and love him now.

Mr. Chandler insisted that our child have a marble stone at his grave in remembrance. A catalog was found among some old magazines and newspapers that he never seemed to want to throw away until they were stacked high in a corner, and I insisted they be thrown out, lest they catch the store on fire. He sat and brooded over what the marker would say, and finally we decided on the one with the little lamb lying down, with his name and dates carved underneath. I wasn't too interested, but Mr. Chandler watched and waited until the day it arrived by wagon. It had been shipped from somewhere in Vermont, I think. Oh, it was a sad day when the men gathered around and planted the stone beside the broken sod where my baby lay. The day was cold and crisp, with a strong north wind that threatened to blow my hat from my head and my skirts high in the air. There were only about a half dozen people there, and Evelyn held my hand while we sang a song and prayed over the stone.

The first visit of the new pastor, Reverend Ethan Watson, didn't go well. He was tall and slender and wore the same dark suit, white collar and black tie as the others, but he wasn't very friendly and didn't approve of music and dancing. The elderly ladies were suspicious from that time on and attended the worship services because he was the only preacher we had. It was on his third trip to the town that the money box was missing.

It was late at night when we closed the store each day, so we put the day's receipts and loose bills and coins in an old metal locked box under the counter. The next morning, Mr. Chandler took the deposit to the bank and marked it in our account. It was on the third visit to the town that Mr. Watson ate dinner with us, and we enjoyed the visit well enough. There was no talk of politics, Egyptian Pharaohs or Jewish Temple Guards. He spoke of the weather, of floods, earthquakes and other catastrophes, and I thought he was describing events in the book of Revelation. We said good night and wished him well, for he was staying with the widow Randall that night and planned to leave early on his visit with the next parish.

Mr. Chandler heard a faint noise in the store and rose to investigate. I was drowsy and half dreaming when I heard a yell and a loud thunk. He lighted a lamp, and there was Mr. Watson on the floor, the money box in his hand, moaning from the lump on his head. I quickly grabbed a robe and ran to the sheriff's office while Mr. Chandler stayed with him. Oh, what excitement that aroused in the town. The preacher, not satisfied with the funds he had received honestly from the parishioners, but to steal the shopkeeper's night deposit! It was unforgivable.

It was sometime during the trial that someone suggested that we needed a permanent pastor, one who was honest and faithful to his flock. To get such a pastor, we needed to build a church building. The rumor grew into a roar of approval, and the building fund was set up in the bank, under the jurisdiction of Mr. Percival Kincannon, the husband of my friend, Caroline Jennings.

The first deposit was made by Mr. Chandler, and he added to it regularly every month. Alice Jennings made the second deposit, and then the pennies, dimes and dollars came in a flood of emotion as the trial continued. The man was found guilty of theft and sentenced to five years in the penitentiary, but it was commuted by the Federal Judge at Fort Sill, who served as the highest authority in the Territory at the time. The town was so angry that if they could have gotten their hands on the preacher, I'm afraid there would have been a lynching. He was safely kept in the guardhouse at the Army post, too far for the citizens of the town to travel. I believe he went to California, or maybe

Oregon.

The church was a small but substantial half-rock, half-wooden edifice with a steeple on top. That was the results of the attempted thievery. Mr. Kincannon Senior donated the money for the bell to toll the daylight hours and celebrations of the town, and it was shipped from a smelter in the East. That building was replaced years later by a larger brick one, but we were proud of our First Methodist Church, bought and built by the town. Each family brought a couple of chairs from home until we'd raised the money for pews. Old Isaac Prichard built them in his shed. The next step was to apply to the Board of Directories of the nearest Methodist Seminary for a permanent pastor, one who was young and enthusiastic, yet compassionate and kind to the children and elders. Three months later, before the church building was finished, Reverend Samuel Moore Raymond arrived on the train from St. Louis, Missouri. He was young and handsome, and loved music and dancing and church socials of all kinds.

Less than a year after his arrival, he was married by the District Bishop, in his own church, to Miss Janice Yancy, the grade school teacher, my friend. I served as her matron of honor, and several of her students attended her as flower girls or ushers. It was a fabulous wedding, and the bell tolled for a long time. The dancing lasted even longer, until we realized that the bride and bridegroom had left in her father's buggy. They took a short wedding trip, and the next Sunday morning, as usual, he was standing in his place near the altar. Janice wore a lovely green linen frock and beamed with joy. The groom grinned in satisfaction, sobered, and preached the longest sermon I believe I've ever heard. We teased him about it for years afterward.

His first funeral service was for our dear Mrs. Alice Jennings, who was struck by lightning in her own backyard while gathering in the washing. It was a sad time for the town, for she was the spark that had given it life during the early years, when hers was the only real house in town. The ranchers, farmers and merchants from near and far filled the new church with their presence, and the yard was full of up-standing citizens who came to pay their respects. Her daughters agreed to have long tables made from sawhorses and covered with bed sheets set up in the churchyard under a tree, and the women brought food for everyone. I've never seen Caroline and Evelyn look so lovely, nor so gracious to their guests. My brother, Thomas, was there, of course, as husband of Evelyn. Caroline, ever the social butterfly, was on the arm of her husband, Percy Kincannon, the banker. He was seen shaking hands with the town council members and the City Marshall. He was later elected mayor of the town when we were, at last, consolidated and incorporated.

Oh, it was a grand occasion, that funeral dinner in the churchyard; our friends and neighbors, and strangers from a far distance came to say farewell to one of the earliest citizens of the town. Old Mack Webster was there, and Neva Fitzsimmons, my father's housekeeper; my father, of course, looking frail and thin; and Dr. Griffith, barely able to walk from his latest bout with the rheumatism, leaning on the arm of his son, Jake, who operated a cattle ranch near the border; and the new Dr. Letson, a dentist, and his pretty wife, Bertha. The Army doctor, Dr. Smith, now retired from the military service, drove over from Mangum, and we were glad to speak with him; he was still handsome and gay, and had a stick of candy for the children, as always. I shamelessly asked his first name, and he told me it was Alfred. He told Mr. Chandler that he'd bought a small farm in Greer County and was growing cotton on it. We were sad to see him go home. There are times in which you share, and it bonds you together forever; such a time was the influenza epidemic in our town.

The greatest surprise of all was the appearance of Reverend Kennedy and his wife, Susie. Oh, it thrilled me to see my old friends. They'd come all the way from Louisiana, and stayed at the hotel for three days, and it was like the old days, so pleased was Mr. Chandler to see him. They talked for hours as they had before, while Susie and I peeled potatoes or baked a pie. One wonderful day, we took a picnic lunch into the country and visited with Janice and her husband, Reverend Raymond. The three men said they wanted to fish in the creek but never put a line in the water; the two preachers shared notes and sermon tips, and my husband, so pleased with each other's conversation; and Susie, Janice and I gossiped and watched our husbands with pride and fellowship. I don't think I've ever seen a more encouraging day as sitting there on a quilt in the open air with my dear friends.

About a year later, the twins, Caroline Kincannon and Evelyn McLean, sent for a stained glass window to be placed high above the altar in memory of their mother. Isaac Pritchard had to have help carving out a place in the wooden wall and lifting it, but it was beautiful. The window had simple multi-colored pieces of glass as a background for a portrayal of Jesus holding a lamb in his arm and a shepherd's staff in the other hand. I gazed at that window and felt calm and peaceful as I watched the light shift through the colors and reflect on the different parts of the room. That was the one thing I regretted about the new, finer sanctuary; there was no place built for the window, and it was sold to another church congregation. But, that was many years later, and hardly anyone was left who remembered Alice Jennings or her daughters.

One day in summer, a cowhand came to tell us Father was dead. He died peacefully in his sleep. It was a simple but well-attended funeral held at the ranch, and we buried him beside my mother and the two unnamed little ones who didn't survive infancy. They were near my brother Richard, who drowned when he was young. We sang the old hymns he loved, the preacher held his speech to a minimum, and we sang some more songs that he liked. The men carefully lifted him into the hole dug for him, for he had requested no coffin, but to be laid uncovered in the soil of his home. Mr. Chandler sent for a few soldiers from Ft. Sill who knew him from his trips there to come and hold a soldier's salute for him. The sound of shots in the air, and the echo of the bugle blowing stayed for many minutes on the quiet scene. People came from miles around on horseback, in buggies and farm wagons. My father was a good man, and of that, I'll say no more.

Thomas, of course, took ownership of the ranch, as had been planned since his birth. Rose didn't come for the funeral but sent a telegram and money for a memorial to him. We debated and discussed what form it should take and finally settled on a scholarship fund to send a child of the town who made good grades to go East to college. Stephen Crum was chosen, and he did us proud, became a doctor and came back to the Territory and took over Dr. Griffith's practice. Eventually, he and Dr. Letson, the dentist, helped build a clinic and hired another doctor and three nurses to assist him. Dr. Crum served the community for over forty years, and we all respected him.

I was given my share of the ranch in Father's will, a small acreage near the northwest section. We built a summer home there but hardly stayed in it. We rented it to one of the cowhands and enjoyed the profit in trips to Virginia to see Mr. Chandler's family and to see Rose and John in Philadelphia.

My first trip to Philadelphia was beyond belief. It was so large, the buildings tall, and the sounds and smells delightful, but it didn't hold the charm for me as did Richmond in Virginia. It was too crowded and too busy for my taste, but Rose loved the excitement, the glamor of the theater and the art museums. She was a charming hostess and a loving wife and mother. Yes, my sister Rose had two children, both boys. It was amusing to watch them play in the yard, and John Beldon was a fine father. We went ice skating in the park, and had a sit-down dinner with a famous actor in the theater at the time, but I don't remember his name. We laughed at the antics of John's younger sister, Becky, and her beau as he courted her with flowers and candy.

I was absolutely mortified when I brushed against a valuable bowl in the hallway and it crashed to the ground. I apologized profusely, but Rose remembered the days of our childhood and said I did it from spite. Mr. Chandler offered to pay for another to replace it, but she wouldn't agree to the suggestion. Poor Rose. She never changed, always self-centered and lovely of face and form.

I always rode the train back to the Territory with a feeling of relief and sadness combined with the love of life one feels when pleased with oneself. Mr. Chandler was my strong shield in those days. He held my hand and fed me salted peanuts and lemonade until I was over the melancholy thoughts of my childhood days with Rose and Thomas and Richard, roaming the hills and dales on my horse, Nellie.

— 6 —

Sadly, the children didn't come to us. Tonight, as I sit in my ninety-fourth year at the rough, scratched wooden desk from Mr. Chandler's office, pen in hand, I remember as clearly as the sky on a summer afternoon those first days and weeks of our marriage. I took my proper place behind the counter of Mr. Chandler's store. What a time I had, learning the names of the items of merchandise and the cost of each piece. I made many mistakes, but Mr. Chandler was patient and kind. He taught me how to order by the gross and by the pound: the canned goods, the sacks of staples and the barrels of cider, as well as the different types of nails and bolts. Oh, the long lists of figures and ink-stained pages in the log books haunt me still. The nights I sat by lamplight at this very desk and totaled figures until my head swam with numbers, while I listened to the crickets chirping and the night sounds of the town.

I can hear as though it were yesterday, the bell over the door jangling as a customer came in. I would rush from the living quarters, draw aside the curtain and greet our neighbors with a smile. He taught me that, my husband, to always smile, even if I felt bad or hated to wait on the nosy gossips or the strict church ladies. He said I had the sweetest smile on earth. It paid off in the end, for the ladies liked to stand in a cluster and discuss the shades of cloth, the new glass fruit jars, or the latest in Paris bonnets.

They didn't come from Paris, France, of course, but it seemed to give them pleasure to think they did. I spent my leisure time sewing ribbons, flowers or feathers to the drab straw bonnets that came by the dozen from St. Louis. I stitched lace on cotton frocks and knitted sweaters and caps and mittens by the thousands for the cold winter weather. It gave me pleasure to see the ladies wear them back to the store. Vanity, I know, but to be a part of the growing town in such a way was nice.

Mr. Chandler was right; the settlers came, and the town grew and grew. Through the years, we watched the youngsters as they rode or walked by the window on their way to school, then before we could blink, they were pairing off and getting married, and a new generation came through our door. In the tenth year of our partnership, the new store that he promised was built, and we moved into a large white house on the edge of town. He brought seedlings from the river bed to plant in the yard for shade and shelter for the birds. I hired a widow lady to cook and to clean. Mrs. Bessie Caruthers, her name was, and she stayed with us about five years and moved to Pottsboro to be with her daughter.

I did see the tall trees, the huge plantations, the lovely flowers and the wide rivers of the Eastern country my mother told me about, but not in Mississippi. I saw the wonderful city of Richmond in Virginia and watched a real live show in a theater in Philadelphia. Mr. Chandler took me with him several times on his journeys to Virginia to see his family and buy supplies. His sisters were haughty and looked at me askance when I said I had ridden my pony with some Indian braves. Of course, that was a big whopper, for the Indians in the Territory mostly had nothing to do with the white girls. I liked to tease them about my backward schooling, but actually, I had as much education as they did, and maybe more, for my mother taught my sister Rose and me more than what was taught in the one-room school in the Territory.

How proud I was to walk the city streets with Mr. Chandler, with my hand on his arm, and know that he was mine. His sisters' husbands were well enough, and his brother in Arkansas was kind, I suppose, but they didn't shine nearly as brightly as my man. I held my head high and twirled my fancy parasol like I was a real lady. How I laughed at the days of my youth when I rode my horse Nellie through the tall grass and herded the cattle into the corrals. If my mother could have seen me in the East, I think she would have been proud of me. I enjoyed helping him select the items for our store, things that we thought the ladies of the prairie would need or want. I would gaze in wonder at the gadgets: a meat grinder; or a new coffee bean crusher; or strange vegetables. We brought back seeds by the hundreds to try in the rich soil of our prairies.

I will never forget the look on Mrs. Alice Jennings' face when I brought her a silver locket on a chain with two places to put her twin daughters' pictures. Caroline and Evelyn were my special friends at home, and Mrs. Jennings was kind to me, always. Evelyn became my dear sister-in-law, and I loved her well.

The names and the dates now appear foggy in my memory, as I sit beside the fireplace in the rocking chair Mr. Chandler had made for my twenty-fifth birthday. The tragedies and triumphs, the laughter and tears, it's all behind me now, and Mr. Chandler rests underneath the great oak tree in the church cemetery beside our precious stillborn son, Amos; the church that he helped build, the stones taken from the quarry outside of town. Twenty-two years we had together, he and I. Just twenty-two short, lovely years.

It was a long illness, and his skin grew pale and soft; his body was racked and thin from the pain. I saw the blue veins of his gnarled hands, the long thin fingers that had worked hard for his wife and his town. I cried all night as he lay so still and lonely-looking on the bed, as the candles sputtered and smoked on the tables. I insisted on that, for I didn't want him to lie in the dark alone. The funeral service was short and the music grand; the journey to the graveyard, cold in the gray light of February, seemed to go so slowly. As the last hymn echoed around the room, the bells in the steeple began to toll the mournful song of death.

I cannot dwell on the days of sadness, for the people expect the store to open in the morning, as usual. Life goes on, as Pastor Kennedy, our dear friend of long ago, said. Days filled with wonder and joy, pleasure and determination. I must close my useless, wandering tale now, for my eyes grow weary and my fingers numb. I will rest awhile, I think. Soon, I'll rise and make a cup of hot tea, sit in my chair on the porch and watch the evening stars come out above the town. Trudy Stripling will come to tuck me in, as she does each evening, then the lights will be turned out, and I'll sleep in the big maple bed where his dear head lay on the pillow closely beside me.

I'll feel once again in my dreams his strong arms and hear the gentle snore that made me feel secure in the night. I'll close my eyes and dream of that night so long ago, our wedding night. Yes, I remember those days spent with Rudolph Chandler, my husband, and the white-washed racket store in which we spent our days. The smell of leather and perfumed oil, the sound of shuffling feet and conversation, and his stooped shoulders as he toted up the figures at this same desk, while I cooked his dinner, are as real to me as the trees he planted and the annual roses that come up in the springtime.

Drat. I've knocked over the ink pot. and the liquid is soaking into the wood. There! I've not ruined the pile of papers as I wiped the last of the ink away; for I wouldn't wish to write it all again. Dick Macon, the editor of the newspaper asked me, the oldest living citizen in the town, to jot down my memories for his Sunday morning edition, to commemorate the seventy-fifth year since the first newspaper was published in the town, and I wouldn't want to disappoint him, for I remember the day his mother brought him, a gangly youngster of five years, into the store the first time. Mr. Chandler handed him a peppermint stick, and his eyes grew wide and sparkled with joy.

Dick Macon. How nicely he has grown into a handsome, successful editor and leading citizen. Maybe, I should tell the story of his farewell to the town before going away to college. That should amuse the readers. I'll wait until tomorrow, for I am so tired . . .

— *Postscript* —

TUESDAY, NOVEMBER 22, 1958

Pioneer Settler Dies in Her Sleep
BY: JAMESON T. CANNON

It is with a great deal of sadness that yours truly, editor of the Post-Dispatch, must report the death of one of our oldest citizens, Mrs. Rudolph Chandler, who along with her gentle giant of a husband, owned and operated the Chandler General Merchandise Store on North Main Street at the corner with Belknap Avenue for many years.

After the death of her husband, Mrs. Chandler continued running the store until it was sold about twenty years ago to its present owner, and the name changed to Farraday's Department Store. The dear lady passed from this world last night during her sleep in the ninety-fifth year of her age. She was a sweet, kind lady, and the people of the town will sorely miss her winning smile and charming manner. She has left no children to mourn her passing, and the remaining estate will go to her nephew, Thomas McLean, Junior, a well-known cattleman of the area. I have been told by the manager that Farraday's store will close on Friday to mark her passing.

Mrs. Chandler came with her family as a small child from Mississippi to this area shortly after the Civil War when wild animals and Indians still roamed the land. She and Mr. Chandler were married for about twenty years and spent their waking hours toiling in the family-owned store. She will be long remembered by those who knew her and benefitted through her service to the community. She was a loyal member of the First Methodist Church and sang in the choir. One of her last deeds was to write a remembrance of the early days for this newspaper for the celebration of our seventy-fifth year, and it will be reprinted, as written in her own style, in the coming Sunday edition.

She was preceded in death by her husband, her parents, a brother, Thomas McLean, Senior, of the T Bar K ranch, a sister, Rose Beldon, wife of the late John Beldon, a longtime attorney in the City of Philadelphia, and a brother, Richard McLean, who drowned in his youth. She is survived by several nieces and nephews. Graveside services will be held on Saturday at 10:00 A.M. in the First Methodist Church Cemetery on Grand Avenue. The church bell will toll her passing at twelve o'clock on Saturday, with a reception held in the Fellowship Hall for those who mourn her passing and the closing of an era. Peace to her soul.

Montana Moon

— *Prologue* —

Montana Territory, June 6, 1891

Dear Sister Willie,

    I take pen in hand to inform you that my beloved wife Margaret passed on the tenth of March of a wasting away fever following a fall from the wagon, leaving only myself, son Nicholas and daughter Prissy to mourn the loss. It's been a bad winter, and the snow remained during the month of February. The mule was especially stubborn on that morning, and I lost control of the reins about midway to the town of Blessing for a shopping trip to the general store. We left the children at home with Hank, the hired hand, or they might have been lost, too. Margaret fell over the side and broke her back. I carefully lifted her to the back of the wagon and drove into town. I left her with the kind Mrs. Robinson, whose husband owns the general store, but she never regained consciousness. We buried her at the edge of town in a plot donated by one of the local merchants for the purpose of a burial ground.
    Please to send me a new wife as soon as one can be

had, for the children need a mother. She must be of high moral character and well educated in the social graces as well as reading, writing, arithmetic and geography. Face and figure are not as important as the fact that she is chaste and untouched by another man and under the age of thirty, for I will not tolerate a whore from the saloons of Chicago. She must be strong and healthy, a good cook, a seamstress, tolerant of animals, and helpful with the outside chores of garden and barn when necessary. She must be willing to stand long periods of loneliness as the area is sparsely settled and there are no near neighbors, as you know from your visits to the ranch. Make sure that she has plenty of clothing and shoes and high topped boots, for the mud is sometimes thick after a rain. A heavy wool coat wouldn't come amiss, since the nights are cold, even in summer. I'm sending two hundred dollars for her transportation and necessities on the trip. There is a process of marriage called "by proxy," legal in this territory for single men to find wives at a distance. Look into the matter, and I will take care of the details at this end upon receiving word from you of an eligible woman.

Please to send toys, clothing, shoes and heavy winter coats for the children. Nicholas is now three and Priscilla is aged ten months. They outgrow their clothes so quickly at this age. They'll need blankets and new bedding, for I've built another room onto the house since your last visit. See that the woman has whatever you think necessary for a young matron in the wilderness of Montana to please her tastes. Some flower seed packets might be useful. I'll send the payment for these supplies when I have sold some of the cattle in the fall.

I remain your loving brother, Lucas.

— 1 —

Elizabeth Thompson gazed out of the train window at the lonely, barren plains through which she was riding. She leaned forward a little when she thought she got a glimpse of a prairie dog town. Yes, there was another mound, with a small animal perched on top. She laughed at the antics of the animals. They would flash their bushy tails in panic and then duck down into the holes. Then, they were gone, and she saw only the fog of smoke from the engine drifting by her window. The hot autumn sun baked the short grass of the fields, and she turned away to look at the passengers seen from her seat.

Across the aisle sat a middle-aged couple. Sometimes the woman would chatter away, but Elizabeth couldn't tell whether the man was listening or not. He'd taken out a newspaper earlier and plunged his head into it. But, the news must not have been satisfactory, for he soon folded it and put it away in a leather case he'd placed at his feet. The woman brought out a large basket with food, and she offered her man a sandwich or a piece of cake. The sight reminded Elizabeth that she was hungry, too.

She leaned down and lifted her own basket from the

floor. She placed it on the seat beside her and took from it her last apple. Withdrawing a small pen knife from the portmanteau at her feet, she peeled the apple in one long curling piece, then cut it into halves, then quarters, and with tiny bites of her front teeth, ate the fruit. She savored the sweet, moist taste of the fruit before she swallowed each piece. She put the peelings and core into a small paper bag and set it back in her basket. She found a cookie and munched on it while gazing out the window. She didn't want the couple to think she was spying on them.

Finished with her repast, Elizabeth stretched as best she could in the seat. There was the squeak of brakes, and she knew they were coming to the next stop on their itinerary. She took out her train guide and saw that there were three more stops before she would be at her own destination: Helena, Montana. From there she was to catch the stagecoach to the small town of Blessing. She thought it was a rather funny name for a town, but guessed the early settlers hadn't deemed it so.

The train stopped, and there was a bustle of activity as a group in front of her rose, collected their belongings and left the train. She could see a few houses out her side window. She couldn't see the station located on the other side of the train without looking at the couple, so she gazed with interest at the ground and the gravel, stones and grassy area around the tracks. There was a buggy parked a few feet away, and she assumed it was waiting for the passengers who were debarking from the train.

A man and a young boy came down the aisle and found seats behind her. The boy sounded excited to be on the train. The man's calm, deep voice reminded him to be polite and sit still. Elizabeth thought it a shame for the man to restrict the boy's enthusiasm, for she'd felt the same way when she'd left Chicago. She was past that excitement now, for she'd been on the train for a whole day. She watched as the train left the station and picked up speed. She leaned her head against the back of the cushioned seat and relived that first hour on the train.

The train had left the Chicago station early in the afternoon, and she'd traveled all night in the darkness. She'd brought a small lap robe to cover herself, and the train attendant had passed around small pillows for the passengers. She was so excited, she couldn't sit still. Every time the train stopped, she looked out her window to watch the people and the buggies. Eventually, sheer exhaustion set in, and she could rest, only to be awakened at the next stop.

Jarred from her thoughts, she saw the attendant come down the aisle and say there was less than an hour to arrival at Helena, and all passengers who were getting off should start gathering their things. The man across the aisle asked the attendant if there would be transportation from the train station to the hotel, and the attendant admitted that there might be one or two taxicabs waiting, but there was no guarantee, since they'd arrive at night. Elizabeth began to worry, for she'd been assured by the ticket agent in Chicago that there'd be no problem going from the train station to the Wells Fargo stage line stop.

She opened her small brown leather bag from her portmanteau and pulled out the travel brochure. Yes, there it was in small print. Transportation would be provided at Helena from the train station to the office of Wells Fargo, where she'd transfer to the stage to Blessing, Montana. There was to be a one-hour layover at Helena, in which a meal would be available at the Majestic Hotel. The list of prices for a hot meal or sandwiches and desserts was provided, as well as various cool drinks. As she began to put the brochure back in her bag, she saw the other piece of folded paper lying next to her small coin purse and comb. Her marriage certificate.

She couldn't resist taking it out, although she'd looked

at it so many times on the train that the folded edges were becoming strained. Elizabeth Jane Perkins to Lucas Frederick Thompson. It was signed by the Catholic priest, Father John Moore, three days before. Of course, Lucas hadn't been in Chicago. He lived on a ranch near Blessing. It was an arranged marriage, put together by Mrs. Wilhelmina Pierce of Chicago, the aunt of Lucas Thompson. Elizabeth folded the certificate and placed it and the brochure from the ticket agent back in her bag and snapped the clasp. She leaned back in her seat and went over the events of the last week once more.

She'd been orphaned at the age of nine when both her parents died of the influenza. Her father was a merchant and left a small legacy, but it was soon lost in the cost of expenses for her care. She'd been placed by the local officials in the Joan Hardesty School for Girls in Chicago, because of her advanced age. It was decided by the local judge and court officials that no one would be willing to adopt a girl of her age. It hadn't been a bad life. She'd been placed in a dormitory with other girls her age and soon had a few friends, one named Selena whom she liked to call Sel. She was assigned kitchen duty, where she at first was the dishwasher and maid. Within a year, she'd been taught to cook and bake. If she occasionally cried in the night from loneliness and grief, no one cared, for all the girls felt the same way. Sometimes, she and her friend Sel talked about their parents and their past life, but as the other girl was two years older, they soon accepted the life they'd been thrust into against their will.

The years drifted by, with girls coming and going, some Elizabeth liked and had fine times with, but others she didn't like. Selena left to accept a teaching post when Elizabeth was fourteen. She'd written a couple of times, but the letters stopped as Sel adjusted to her new life. Before she was quite aware of the time, Elizabeth turned eighteen and was assigned as teacher to the younger girls. She liked that job better than kitchen duty. She stood at the head of the class and looked at the audience of young girls, and it gave her a feeling of power and achievement. She enjoyed teaching, for she learned so much more herself, while preparing lessons for the class.

A girl of average height and form, Elizabeth had turned into a full-figured woman before the age of twenty. She talked to the court officials the previous year about leaving the orphanage since she was the oldest resident in the school, but was turned down. They had asked what she would do if she left, and she had said proudly that she could sew, cook, teach or work in a boarding house as a maid. Mrs. Hardesty testified that she was a valuable teacher in her school, so her request for release from the court jurisdiction was denied.

A month ago, Elizabeth had gone with two of the other girls to the "Afternoon Tea" where the older girls were taught manners and deportment. She'd been going to the teas for five years, so her manners were good. She laughed at the jokes of the male guests, and passed around the plates of dainty iced cakes and cups of red punch. On rainy days, she helped the ladies with their coats and hats, and their bags and galoshes.

She was introduced to Mrs. Wilhelmina Pierce and her husband Samuel. They were a middle-aged couple with gray hair. She dressed in the latest style in silks, with a black straw hat on her head, it being the last of August. Samuel Pierce was a portly man who smelled of liquor and tobacco. One of the younger girls coughed as Mr. Pierce walked by, but they had been carefully taught not to notice such things in polite society, and the sound was quickly hushed.

The other two girls were her friend Lilith Grey who had come to the orphanage only a year before and Sally

McQuire, who was a silly girl. Mrs. Hardesty told Elizabeth to keep a special eye out for Sally for she was sometimes clumsy and spilled the punch in a person's lap. At first, since she was watching Sally, Elizabeth didn't notice that Mrs. Pierce was watching her. When she did notice, she became embarrassed and almost spilled the tray of cups herself.

Turning again to the portly gentleman, Elizabeth saw Mrs. Hardesty give her a sharp look. Afraid that she would cause offense in some manner, she finished passing the fancy cakes and moved to the outer circle of guests. Joan Hardesty had a way of looking out of her sharp blue eyes at a girl that set fear in their hearts. She'd started the school when she herself had been abandoned by her husband and needed an occupation. She called herself a widow, but all the girls knew that she'd been divorced by her husband. Elizabeth heard the gossip from the new girls, but she never responded, for the lady had been good to her through the years she'd been in the custody of the court system.

When the tea was over, Elizabeth returned to her room in the dormitory wing of the building. Since she was now a teacher and an adult, she had her own small but starkly bare room. There was nothing but a bed, a wardrobe for her clothes, and a desk with a ladderback chair in her room. There were several shelves where she kept her precious books and knickknacks she'd collected through the years on the field trips into the out-of-doors along the lake shore: a couple of pieces of smooth sea glass from Lake Michigan, a few pretty rocks, and a feather from a male cardinal that brought a touch of red color into the drab room.

Minerva Hutchins, one of the younger girls, came to the door and knocked, then entered without an invitation. "Miss Perkins, you're wanted in the office, right away, Mrs. Hardesty said." She backed out of the room as though she would catch a disease if she lingered any longer.

Oh, my! thought Elizabeth. I've done something to cause offense, but she couldn't think what she'd done. She made her way down the long hallway and across the outer courtyard to the matron's office. She knocked on the door and was told to enter.

The room seemed to be filled with people, but no, there were only five people inside the office, Mrs. Hardesty, Wilhelmina and Samuel Pierce, the Judge in charge of her case, and a Miss Hammond who was her case worker. Elizabeth's heart started to pound so loudly she was sure someone could hear it. She stepped into the room and was told to sit by the matron of the orphanage. She acknowledged the individuals in the room by name as she'd been taught. She sat at the edge of her chair, looking in a panic toward Miss Hammond, for she surely would've warned her if she'd transgressed against the court officials.

"Miss Perkins, circumstances have changed since we spoke with you last year about your residence in the school. It's been called to my attention by Mrs. Hardesty that you have now achieved your twenty-first year, is this correct?" Elizabeth turned toward the judge, and admitted that her birthday was in May of this year.

"Mrs. Pierce has come to us with a special request, which the court is prepared to grant. I've prepared the papers to be filed in the courthouse releasing you into the custody of Mr. and Mrs. Pierce for the time being." With that statement, Judge Bigelow rose and leaned over the desk and signed his name to several sheets of papers. It was witnessed by Miss Hammond and Mrs. Hardesty, and Mr. and Mrs. Pierce signed as well. Elizabeth was told to come forward and sign her name on two of the papers. The judge and Miss Hammond shook her hand, wished her well and left the office.

Elizabeth was bewildered. Did this mean that she was no longer a ward of the court? That she was free to leave the orphanage? Where would she go? What would she do?

She caught Joan Hardesty's eyes. She saw understanding there. Mrs. Hardesty had long told her she was her favorite pupil, but that one day Elizabeth's future would be taken out of her hands. Even the matron of the school was only one person in the hierarchy over the school, and she had no more authority than to feed, clothe, and teach the girls, then of course to let them go when the time came. The judge and the case workers had more authority than Mrs. Hardesty. Now that she was twenty-one, Elizabeth knew she had remained at the school as long as she would be allowed.

She felt a heavy cloud of doubt settle over her. She returned to her seat and folded her hands in her lap to keep them from trembling. She turned politely when the matron of the school started talking.

"Elizabeth, we shall hate to see you go, for you've been a wonderful student and teacher, but you are now released into the custody of Mrs. Pierce, so I'll let her explain the situation." She shook Elizabeth's hand formally and left the office with a heavy tread, her footsteps echoing down the hallway.

Elizabeth looked at Mrs. Hardesty's back as she walked out of the room. She'd been her friend and mentor. What was she to do now? She turned to Mrs. Pierce as she heard her clear her throat.

Wilhelmina Pierce took a folded paper from her handbag. She glanced at it for a moment as though to gain inspiration, then looked at her husband, but he simply shrugged his shoulders, as if to say it was her problem. Elizabeth looked from one to the other, without understanding what had just taken place in the office.

"Ah, Miss Perkins, Elizabeth, I've been observing you for several days without your knowledge. For that I beg your pardon, but I needed to know something of your character and background before I moved on this matter. I interviewed the judge, Miss Hammond and several of the other students and teachers, and they've agreed that you have the qualities I find necessary to fulfill the request of my brother." She stopped speaking and looked at the paper again.

Elizabeth looked at the paper, too. What secret did it hold that impacted her and her life? This lady had been observing her? When? Where? Had she watched through a key hole while she taught her classes? What had her friends said about her?

"You see, Elizabeth, my brother, Lucas Thompson, has recently lost his wife in an accident, and he needs help with his young children, a son, age three, and a baby daughter, thirteen months."

Ah, Elizabeth thought. She was being offered the job of teacher or governess to two children. She breathed a sigh of relief. Yes, she could do that. She was a good teacher.

"My brother lives on an isolated ranch in Montana. There are no schools available for miles around the area. He needs someone of your experience with children of all ages, and with your education and character."

"You want me to be governess to his children? But, surely, they're too young to attend classes at age three and thirteen months. They must need a nursemaid, not a teacher. I have no experience with babies or children younger than school age."

"I see that I haven't made myself clear on the matter. My brother doesn't need a teacher, but someone to be with the children constantly while he's working outside with the horses and cattle, a hard, physical undertaking that demands his whole attention."

Wilhelmina paused, and after a moment, a smile toyed with her lips. She gazed at her husband, who nodded his head in understanding. She pressed the paper against the table top.

"What my brother needs is a wife. I've become convinced that you would be a perfect mate for my brother Lucas. He'll appreciate your full figure. I've never known him to date a skinny, bony girl. His first wife, Margaret was slender, but he'd fallen in love with her." She smiled, but quickly placed her hand over her mouth.

Elizabeth was horrified! She'd been chosen for her physical form, not her education or kitchen skills?

"A wife? Did you a say a wife? How can this be? I've never met your brother. He lives in Montana, you say?" Elizabeth couldn't believe Mrs. Pierce really meant that she should marry a stranger; a rancher with cattle and horses? She'd never been outside Chicago, except to tour the area and go boating with the other girls on Lake Michigan. She knew nothing about animals.

"Yes, you see, my brother's a lonely man. There are no neighbors to speak of, and only one hired man living on the ranch. He needs a woman of education and social qualifications such as you to train the children in the ways of the world. To teach them not only their letters and numbers, but also how to comport themselves in public, how to dress appropriately, and how to become well-rounded citizens of the world."

"But, marriage to a stranger? Couldn't I just live on the ranch without marriage?" Elizabeth saw the shocked expression on her new guardian's face and knew the answer. She took a quick glance at Mr. Pierce and saw the amusement in his eyes. She covered her mouth and gasped. Of course, she thought, the scandal that such an arrangement would cause in the town; a single woman living with two men on an isolated ranch in the middle of Montana. It was unthinkable. Wilhelmina Pierce peered at Elizabeth as though she were some kind of experiment under the microscope. Elizabeth blushed and looked at the floor. She barely remembered not living in the orphanage. She knew nothing of social life. She quickly tried to explain to her tormentor, but she got nowhere. It seemed that Mrs. Pierce had decided on her for the business, and she was trapped, for the judge had passed custody of her person to Mrs. Pierce.

Before she could protest further, Mrs. Pierce suggested that Elizabeth go to her room and pack her bags. Of course, she had no luggage, so her things were packed in paper bags and in a bed sheet-wrapped bundle. She carefully wrapped her sea glass, pretty stones and the feather to protect them, and placed them in a bag of their own that she carried in her hand.

— 2 —

Within the hour, she was gazing in awe at the bedroom assigned to her in the magnificent mansion on the outskirts of Chicago. The room was large, with a bed covered with a pink-and-green spread, and a carpet so thick her feet sank into the plush texture as they had sunk in the sand when she went to the beach on field trips. The luxury of having her own bath was overwhelming, and she sank into the sweet smelling sudsy water with a feeling of unreality. She pinched herself to see if she was dreaming.

Dinner that evening was served in a large dining room built for at least twenty people. But, there were only Mr. and Mrs. Pierce and herself. Roast beef, carrots, onions, potatoes, mustard greens, corn on the cob, fresh butter on bread and apple pie for desert. Servants were used to fetch and carry the food and wine around the table. Elizabeth had never tasted wine, and wasn't quite sure that she liked it. She mimicked the other people, for she was out of her depth. It was fine to say that she had social experience when she simply passed around cups of punch or coffee, and plates of iced cakes, but she'd never been waited on by servants or eaten at such a splendid table, with real flowers in the center.

She came back down to earth quickly when Samuel Pierce left the women in the withdrawing room and went to his club to play cards with his gentlemen friends. Wilhelmina explained to Elizabeth that she was not to expect such service or luxury when she arrived at her brother's house in Montana, for he lived in a much smaller manner, and no neighbors lived nearby. The house was wooden with simple furniture, a large fireplace and a tin roof. The kitchen had a wood-fired range for cooking, however, and the toilet was outside. There was no electricity, and Lucas used kerosene lanterns or candles. Water was taken from a windmill-driven well in the backyard, or the creek that flowed near the house. Wilhelmina had only been there twice, she confessed, so couldn't describe it adequately. Suffice it to say, she admitted, her brother lived in poverty.

Oh, my! Elizabeth wondered why Lucas Thompson had chosen such a simple life when his sister had so much in material possessions. She was afraid to ask. Instead, she asked questions about his person and his character. She was told that he was very tall, had dark hair and eyes, slender build and worked outside every day with the cattle and horses. He'd attended college and trained to be a lawyer, but had chosen to live in the wilderness. She began to suspect that there was a darker motive behind the change in lifestyle, but didn't probe further.

The next day, she was taken to one of the largest mercantile stores and told to choose simple clothing and shoes, a pair of boots, and a warm winter coat. They bought clothing for the children, toys, books, papers and pencils, and water colors. The boxes and bags were dumped on her bed and repacked in the new luggage, boxes and a large trunk. She gazed in wonder at it all, but was still not prepared to marry a stranger for such things.

Downstairs, after dinner, she again tried to confront

Wilhelmina with her protest that she couldn't marry a stranger. She couldn't live in the wild country of Montana, but the older lady gave her a stare that would have shriveled a stone and told her the decision was already made. She'd written to her brother to arrange a marriage by proxy with him. Naturally, Elizabeth had to be told what a marriage by proxy meant. Since the Pierce family was Roman Catholic, the priest would explain the traditions of the church to her.

The next day, feeling emboldened in her new clothes, Elizabeth again attempted to persuade Wilhelmina of her unwillingness to marry her brother, but was told with a sharp glare that the judge had placed her in the older woman's custody, and she would do what she was told or be thrown out on the streets to find her own way in the world. She humbly bowed her head and agreed that she would accept her future life with gratitude.

For the next two weeks, Elizabeth attended regular classes with younger students on the duties and responsibilities of married life. She was to obey her husband in all things, dress modestly, allow him access to her physical person without protest, cook, clean and bear his children. She was drilled so thoroughly that she began to think that married life was a penance for her previous life of luxury in the orphanage. She enjoyed her short time living in the Pierce home and took in the sights and sounds of Chicago, visited its libraries and rode on the trolley cars, but never alone. Wilhelmina was her constant companion, or one of the maids accompanied her when she left the house. In the third week, she knew why. A telegram arrived from Lucas Thompson that the marriage date had been arranged and transportation settled to the satisfaction of everyone.

Except Elizabeth, who still vehemently protested the marriage in her heart, but knew that no one would listen to her complaints. She had been painfully taught that obedience was a virtue, and disobedience was a sin.

On a bright September day, she was taken to a doctor's office, where she was given a thorough examination of her person, including the invasive evidence that she was a virgin. She was humiliated, but was told by the doctor that it was purely routine and necessary for the protection of her groom's reputation. She was given no respite from the degradation that she endured that day. She thought seriously of running away, but she had no money or friends except those at the orphanage, and she was sure they couldn't help her.

On the seventeenth of September, she stood with Samuel Pierce as the representative of Lucas Thompson and was married by proxy. It was an awkward affair. Lucas used the telephone at the general store in Blessing, Montana. The sound was squeaky and weak with static crackling over the wire. His voice seemed deep and masculine. She leaned forward and spoke into the telephone with a clear, bell-like tone, but she wasn't happy. As she spoke her vows, she looked around at the audience, Samuel and Wilhelmina Pierce, a lawyer named Jasper Hastings, who had negotiated with the judge to allow her release from the orphanage, his wife Abigail, and two of Wilhelmina's society friends, sisters Anna and Bettina Watson, who whispered and giggled like school girls, to be used as witnesses to such an unusual event.

The priest stood in his formal attire as representative of the church and officiated. Wilhelmina bought Elizabeth some yellow and white roses and greenery to hold in her hands. It was totally unnecessary, since the groom didn't get to see them, or her in the pale yellow dress. Elizabeth thought it was a kind gesture. A ring was presented and placed on her finger by the priest. And, it was done. The guests went into the dining area and were served a splendid luncheon, with cake and wine.

Two days later, Elizabeth Perkins, now Thompson, came out of her trance, raised her head and noticed that the train had stopped. There was one more station before she arrived at Helena, and she was beginning to feel pains in her stomach not caused by hunger. She was nervous. What if there was no transportation from the station to the hotel? She had a mountain of luggage, trunks, bags and boxes, all taken care of in Chicago by Samuel Pierce, but she had no one in this place to help her. What if Lucas Thompson had changed his mind and left her at the station?

There was no need to worry, however, for as soon as the train stopped and she stepped down, the attendant announced that her ride was ready for her at the station. The wagon was loaded with her possessions, and a grizzled old man with a gray beard helped her aboard the seat and climbed up himself. Taking the reins of the mule, he guided it to the front of the hotel. She was told to enter the door, and he would carry her things to the stage station. Later, he would return for her when it was time for the stage to pull out. She was grateful for the help and gave him a silver coin for a tip. He grinned and pulled away from the hotel portal.

She saw the middle-aged couple who'd sat across from her on the train giving her a speculative look, as though she were royalty. She smiled and entered the hotel. An attendant came forward and led her into a dining room, where she was given a menu and told a waiter would soon be with her. She ate a meal of chicken and dumplings, but she could hardly digest it, she was so excited. Less than an hour later, she was handed into the coach for the last leg of her journey. She would be traveling several hours, she was told, and given a blanket and a pillow by the stage driver. She was beginning to think she must be royalty, she'd been treated so kindly. She propped the pillow behind her head, covered herself with the blanket and was soon asleep, she was so tired.

She was jerked awake by a bump in the road, causing the stage to tilt a bit, then right itself. She heard some cursing from the driver but disregarded it. She looked at the only other person in the coach, a young man dressed in a natty store-bought suit like those worn by Samuel Pierce. She didn't speak to him, and he ignored her, gazing out the window at the gathering darkness. The sun was low on the horizon, and she was certain she would soon reach her destination, for the horses were traveling fast. She began to speculate on whether she would be met by her husband or the hired hand.

She could feel her nervousness mounting. She imagined giant goldfish swimming in her belly. She felt overly warm so removed the blanket, but was instantly cold, so put it back again. She held tightly to the chain handle of her leather handbag. She ran her fingers up and down the length of the chain, feeling its smooth surface and the ring connections through her kid gloves. She gulped in surprise as she saw the man looking at her. She quickly dropped her gaze to the floor.

"You must be Mrs. Thompson." The well-dressed man seated across from her gazed out the window. "I heard about Lucas marrying again. Everyone in the county is wondering what you look like." He turned, then, and looked into her eyes.

"Everyone?" She squeaked. She was surprised that the stranger spoke to her of personal matters.

"Everyone. Can't be more than a hundred people living here abouts. Came through last month and was told that Lucas Thompson had bought himself a new wife to take care of his young'uns." He seemed to be watching closely to see how she would react. "What's your name and where you from?"

"Elizabeth Thompson, and I'm from Chicago." She

was wishing now she hadn't responded to the man's questions. Wasn't that one of the things that the priest had warned her about? Talking to strangers? What did he mean that Lucas had bought his wife?

"Chicago, huh? I was in Chicago onct; went for a convention of salesmen. My name's Jedediah Masters; everyone calls me Jed. Nice, friendly city, Chicago. I came from New Orleans, and sometimes I wish I hadn't come. It's a lonely, isolated place, Montana. Lucas will be glad to see you. That hired hand of his isn't much of a cook. I've eaten his food before. Are you a good cook?"

"Yes, I believe I can cook." Elizabeth noticed that the coach was slowing down, and a rider was seen out of her window.

"I sell farm equipment and leather harnesses to the local farmers and ranchers. You'll see more of me in the future. There's your husband's hired man, now. He must have come out of town to meet the stage." He leaned out the window and gestured to the horseback rider, who came in closer to the stage.

The stagecoach came to a stop. The horseback rider lowered himself from the horse. He came to the door and spoke to the man. "Jed, didn't know it was time for you to come back around. We expected you next month. Someone in there with you?" He opened the door as he was speaking.

Elizabeth dropped the blanket from her shoulders and began to fold it neatly, but it was taken from her hands and thrown on the floor. She thought the stranger presumptuous to grab the blanket off her person like that. Jed picked it up and laid it on the seat beside him. He grinned, but she turned to the stranger when he spoke.

"You Elizabeth Thompson?" the rider asked; his face in the open door. He smelled of fresh air and horse. He turned his head aside and let fly a stream of tobacco juice.

She drew back in disgust, but tried not to let the men see her reaction.

"Yes, I'm Elizabeth."

"I'm Hank Mitchell. Lucas sent me to fetch you. Wanted to see if you was here afore I git the wagon from the livery stable. See you in town." The rider withdrew from the door and shut it. He yelled something to the driver, and the coach started forward again. Elizabeth looked at Jed across the space of the coach with a question in her eyes.

"Aye, that's Hank. You'll get used to him. There's no harm in him, just primitive in manners. He's part Indian, I've heard tell. A hard worker, and sleeps in his own cabin near the barn. I've heard he's good with the children, too." He handed her the blanket, and she wrapped it around her shoulders again.

About half an hour later, the coach pulled to a stop in front of a large building. Elizabeth craned her neck to look up at the sign that read Robinson's General Store. Several men were waiting on the wooden porch in front of the structure. One of them was the man who had approached the coach earlier. He moved closer and opened the door. The young man stepped out first. "Evening, Hank, good to see you again. How's the cattle business?"

"Tolerable. Just tolerable, had a bad winter. You staying in town tonight or headed out to the widow Jones' place?" He laughed loudly and spit a trail of tobacco juice at the coach's front wheel.

Elizabeth watched as Jed laughed at the question and dodged the tobacco juice but didn't answer. He went to the back of the coach, removed his own luggage, and with a jaunty wave at the other men, walked toward the livery. The men gathered on the porch now moved closer and stared at the woman sitting in the coach. One of the men started lifting down the trunk and bags from the coach. He had a cap on his head that said Wells Fargo.

Hank Mitchell, as though nothing had happened, handed her down from the coach and inquired if she had a fine trip. Her face as warm as a freshly baked biscuit, she replied that it had been pleasant enough. He closed the door behind her and held her elbow to guide her to the wagon standing by the side of the porch. She quickly looked around but didn't see much in the gathering dusk. A few houses, the store, the livery and another building that might be a hotel or saloon, she couldn't tell.

Hank helped his boss's wife onto the wagon seat, then went back to get the blanket and pillow. The stage driver lifted her luggage from the top of the coach, and Hank helped him. They gathered the rest of her things from the baggage rack in the back of the coach. As they worked, the Wells Fargo agent brought the fresh horses forward and exchanged them for the next relay of the trip, creating a momentary kerfuffle. It soon righted itself, and the men loaded her belongings onto the farm wagon, and the driver climbed aboard the stage and off he went into the lonely night.

Hank talked to the storekeeper for a few more moments and came back to his wagon, tied his saddle horse on the back and climbed aboard. Elizabeth was cold, whether from the night air or the excitement of being so near her destination, she didn't know, but wrapped the blanket around her shoulders and the wagon started moving.

"Is Mr. Thompson home with the children?" She thought that was a safe topic. Hank sat like a stone and didn't answer. She began to grow upset. She decided that she would let him be the first to speak. Goodness, she'd come hundreds of miles, and the hired hand didn't even want to speak to her. She decided he must be trying to concentrate on his driving.

It was full dark now, with only a sliver of a moon in the sky. She remembered that one of her students had told her that when the moon was in that position, it meant that it was holding water. She'd laughed at the old wives' tale, but now she saw only open space and a sky filled with stars and wondered if it was true. She was disappointed that she was unable to see the landscape in the darkness. She didn't think she had ever seen so many stars. Hank let flow a stream of tobacco juice over the side, and the wind blew it to the ground.

"Some people think I got nothing to do but visit."

Elizabeth glanced over at the driver, thinking he must be speaking to her. They'd come some distance, and the silence was almost deafening. The only sound was the clip, clop of the horse's hooves and the creak of the wagon springs. Hank seemed to be muttering to himself, and she sat still, trying to be especially quiet, hoping he would think her asleep.

"Got to go by instinct with it so dark. Don't know that I approve of this proxy marriage business. Don't seem right to me. Boss done got himself a looker though. Guess he'll be pleased enough. I hope she can cook. I'm right hungry and us not even close to home. Get along there, Fair Maiden. Take your lead." He clicked his tongue in his cheek to get the horse moving faster.

Elizabeth smiled. She supposed the man lived alone so much that he'd gotten into the habit of speaking his thoughts out loud. She puzzled over this new situation. If the hired hand didn't approve of the marriage, it was possible the neighbors didn't either. No wonder the men had stared at her when she got out of the coach. There was no going back to Chicago. She'd have to take each day as it came. She wondered what the children were like. Would they like her?

She looked up at the stars. She thought of Mrs.

Hardesty and the girls back in the orphanage. It was hard to imagine. She was in Montana and sitting beside a man who didn't approve of proxy marriages. She took a deep breath of the cool, night air and sighed. She snuggled in her warm blanket and was soon asleep.

She awoke when the wagon came to a complete stop. She stretched her neck to get the kinks out, for she had let her head drop forward in her sleep. She looked around and saw the buildings of the ranch. At least, she assumed it was the ranch, for why would he travel further in the dark? It seemed to be in the middle of a forest, since she could see tall trees all around the house. Hank dropped from the wagon, came around and helped her from the seat. Behind him there was a tall man standing in the glow from the lighted house. A medium-size dog stood at his side. She could see only his silhouette, but assumed this must be her husband.

The man walked toward her, and she felt silly standing awkwardly near the wagon. He stared at her figure. Her head barely came to his chin, and she wondered if he thought her too fat, but maybe he would blame it on the layers of clothing, for the weather was still cool. He took her elbow and helped her up the steps and through the door into the lighted room.

"Damn," he muttered under his breath, looking away from her. "Is she pregnant?"

Elizabeth was aghast. Did he think she hadn't ears? She was respectable, by all that was good and holy! However, he wasn't finished with his suppositions as he slammed the door shut and turned on her, like a wild tiger.

"Has Willie sent me some whore from the gutter? I specifically said I wanted a virgin. Damn it!" The dog whined at the door, and he snapped his finger at it, calling, "Hush, Joey. You don't belong inside."

He grimaced, and Elizabeth decided he hadn't meant

to be cruel. Maybe she'd misunderstood him. She considered her words carefully.

"I am a virgin. I have papers for you from your aunt, Mr. Thompson." She stood stiff and bold and defiant.

He stared at her and blinked as though coming out of a trance, then pushing her before him with a hand in her back, walked straight through the living area and into the kitchen.

She had only a glimpse of a sofa, a large chair and a few small tables in the living area, before she was in the over-heated kitchen. Her eyes watered in the bright light. On one side, near the back door, was an iron, wood-burning cook stove, with a basket of kindling beside it. She barely had time to notice the shelves of utensils and dishes, before her husband turned her around and started removing her hat and coat. He backed up and put the coat on a peg near the stove, then hung the hat over it.

"Did Willie tell you what I need a wife for?" The man stared into her eyes, and then looked over her, taking in every curve and joint. She wanted to flee in embarrassment, but stood as calmly as she could.

"Willie?" She decided to look at him in the same manner in which he was perusing her body. So, this was Lucas Thompson; brown hair, brown eyes, closely shaven chin, tall, slender hips, with long legs. His face was craggy and nut brown, she assumed from working in the sun all day. There was a strip of pale skin on the forehead where his hat covered it. His head came up to her face at her question. He frowned.

"My sister, Wilhelmina. Did she tell you I need a woman to take care of the children? To teach them manners and their letters? She wrote me that you can cook and sew and color with paints. I don't care for such stuff myself, but the children need a good education. All I need is a good meal on the table and a willing woman in my bed.

Did the doctor find you chaste? I told her I didn't want no gutter woman, but a nice clean female, with refinement." He let his eyes wander over her body again. He gestured for her to sit on the bench near the table.

She sat, amazed at the length of his speech. She'd begun to wonder if he was going to speak to her at all. He seemed to be angry about something. Was he disappointed in her appearance?

"Ah, yes. I submitted to a doctor's examination. I have letters for you." She took a couple of papers from her handbag and gave them to him. She sat on the edge of the bench as her husband looked first at the marriage certificate signed by the priest and the registration of the marriage by the clerk of the court. He opened the letter from his sister and read it.

The frown grew on his face, and Elizabeth began to get nervous. What had Wilhelmina written? He moaned out loud. He looked at her, and she lifted her head in defiance. She would not let him intimidate her.

"See what my sister has written!" He tossed the letter on the table, angrily opened the door to the stove and threw a piece of wood in before shutting it with a loud clang. He put a finger to his mouth and muttered, "Damn." He must have burned it on the door.

Elizabeth had no sympathy for him as she picked up the letter and began to read it. She was horrified as she read the note, and she felt warmth wash over her face and knew it must be pink from embarrassment. Wilhelmina had written how she remembered that he always chose plump women from the village when he courted them before he met his wife. She hoped he would be pleased with her choice. Elizabeth didn't finish the letter, but threw it on the table. She looked up to see him gazing at her with a strange look in his eyes.

"I can't tell from that drab gray dress you wear, but you

must have your chest bound, if you are as well-endowed as Willie says, and not just fat." She heard him mutter as he turned away "Clearly women wear girdles and lots of petticoats today, but this one seems round and firm. I'll find out later. Damn Willie, to tease me in this way."

He turned to the letter from the doctor. He looked at it for a long time and coughed. He handed it to her to read. She saw that it was a formal declaration that he had examined the girl in question and found her undefiled and her body well-formed. He saw no reason why she couldn't produce a large number of children with good nutrition and healthy exercise. Her lungs and heart were in perfect condition for a woman of twenty-one years.

Elizabeth laid the doctor's letter on the table beside the other papers. She wanted to cry, but she refused to show weakness before this strange man who was her husband. She was beginning to agree with Hank that proxy marriages were not a good idea. She was bound to Lucas Thompson by the law, but her soul was intact, as was her pride. He couldn't take those from her unless she allowed it. She stood straight and tall, waiting for him to decide what he would do now.

Lucas folded all the papers, except the marriage certificate, and put them in his pocket. He handed her the certificate, for that should be her property. He turned to the large pot on the stove and dipped some beef stew and potatoes onto a plate and put it on the table in front of her. He took a few biscuits from the oven where he had kept them warm and put them on her plate. He poured her a cup of coffee.

"You're probably tired from your journey; best eat and go to bed. The bedroom's down that hall." He pointed to a door on the opposite side of the room from the stove. "I'll help Hank with your luggage and then check the animals and be back in a few minutes." Lucas was gone without another word.

Elizabeth stared at the plate of stew for a moment and turned the ring around her finger several times. She put the certificate of marriage back in her handbag. She knew what was expected of her from the lecture she'd received from the priest, but she wasn't sure she was prepared for such an abrupt introduction from her husband. Of course, he would expect to consummate the marriage, but he hadn't said anything about the children or the house or ranch. She had somehow expected a few days to get acquainted with everything.

She picked up the fork and began to eat, for she was hungry. The stew was bland and tasteless; the biscuits hard and cold. The coffee was good, however, and it warmed her. She ate all the food then took the dishes to the enamel pan on the counter and washed them. Taking a linen towel from a rack, she dried them thoroughly and placed them on the shelf beside others like them. She saw nothing else she could do in the kitchen, so picked up her bag and walked to the door which Lucas had pointed out. He hadn't indicated where the toilet was, so she cautiously opened the back door and saw an outhouse a few yards from the house. A few clouds drifted near the moon, and it seemed to the woman that a million stars shone in the sky as she came back to the house.

The bedroom was cool and dark. There didn't seem to be many furnishings, a bed, a table with a lamp and a wardrobe for their clothes. A few shelves on one wall were full of objects, but she couldn't see them in the dark. She lit the lamp and looked about her. The shelves contained books, a clock and a picture of an elderly couple and two children: Wilhelmina and Lucas and their parents. Elizabeth quickly undressed and washed her face and upper body, then donned the pretty white cotton gown that Wilhelmina insisted she wear on her wedding night. She crawled into the bed and gazed with trepidation at the ceiling, waiting for her husband to appear, her body stiff and straight in the huge bed, and her mind active as she reviewed the events of the last hour.

— 3 —

Elizabeth awoke the next morning before the sun peeped over the horizon. She heard the crow of a rooster near the half-open window. A dog barked, and she assumed it was Joey from the previous night. He was an outside dog and probably barked at anything and nothing. A cool breeze was blowing in, and she snuggled under the heavy covers of the bed. She realized that she was alone in the bed, but knew that her husband had lain beside her, for the faint lingering scent of a male body remained behind. She went back over the events of the previous night and could think of nothing that might have offended Lucas, but remembered him saying that she was there to teach his children. She tried to recall what Wilhelmina had said about her brother's loneliness, but that didn't explain his behavior, for wouldn't he have come to her if that were so? Accustomed to work and loneliness herself, she rose and donned a fresh, clean gingham dress from her portmanteau. She brushed her long hair, braided it into a rope and pinned it on top of her head, gazing at herself in the small oval mirror on the wall. She sighed and thought to herself, she was a very good teacher, and if that was what he wanted, than she would do her best to please him.

The house seemed much larger than she'd been expecting from Wilhelmina's description. From what she had discovered in the dark so far, the outside was a simple clapboard, rambling style, badly in need of paint. There was a large screened-in porch with a few holes in the screening. At one end stood a washing machine with a wooden-handled crank and a device for flushing out the excess water. Two empty galvanized tubs stood nearby, and a small table held bars of lye soap and a lantern. From this angle, she could see the chimney was made of multi-colored rocks of various sizes and shapes, put together with clay mortar. A small verdant area to the side looked to be a badly neglected flowerbed, overgrown with weeds.

Carrying the lamp, she moved through the house from room to room. There were two bedrooms upstairs, and two downstairs, with the staircase located in the central hallway between the lower bedrooms on the left and the kitchen and dining area on the right. Inside, the floors were bare in the living area and squeaked when walked upon. The boards were wide and needed scrubbing. She ducked her head into the parlor and saw her bags and trunk in the living area. She was appalled by the dust and clutter; but in the corner was a huge fireplace, with a large rustic beam for a mantle. There seemed to be some framed pictures and knickknacks on the mantle, but she didn't take the time to examine them. Above the mantle was a large, faded painting of far-distant, snow-topped mountains, with a green meadow of various colored spring flowers in front, and she gave a small gasp of pleasure. The walls of the room were covered with water-stained, grotesque, flowered paper, and from the ceiling hung a few strips of brown sticky paper covered with dead flies.

She shuddered, went into the kitchen and lit a second lantern. The cupboards were rustic, the floor covered in faded brown linoleum worn thin in places by many footsteps. She gazed with critical eyes around the kitchen and moved to look more closely at the kitchen stove. It was not very different from the one on which she had cooked in the orphanage. She picked up some kindling and a few sheets of newspaper in the basket and lit the fire. She glanced around to familiarize herself with the objects and supplies necessary for her job as cook. She found the pump that pulled water from the pipes elsewhere in the house. She filled the coffee pot and the kettle. She saw a small door and found the root cellar with vegetables and meat hanging from hooks in the ceiling. There were barrels and boxes and tins of food. She found some potatoes, onions, bacon and flour.

A few minutes later, she heard the chatter of a child's voice. She went into the room next to her own and found a small boy sitting in the middle of his cot, talking to his baby sister, who lay in a cradle near the window. He stopped and stared at her. She stared back, then quickly told him her name was Elizabeth and went to the cradle. The little girl, Priscilla, looked up at her with soft brown eyes. The little boy's eyes were blue. She asked him where his clothes might be. He pointed to a chest with drawers in the far corner. She opened a drawer and found a boy's garments. She collected what she needed, came back to the boy and placed the garments on his bed. She opened another drawer and found the girl's napkins and dresses.

She made a fast trip to the kitchen to make sure her food wasn't burning and dressed the children. She used her experience at the orphanage to talk to them in a singsong voice, explaining that she was their new mother and what she was doing in their home. When they were both dressed, she returned to the kitchen and soon had biscuits in the oven, light and round and slightly sticky. Fried bacon, perfectly crisp, and jam and marmalade were placed on the table for sweets. There was a large skillet of fried potatoes and onions, and squishy golden yellow eggs.

She heard a noise at the door and felt a gust of wind. She looked around.

"Good morning, gentlemen." She smiled, although she thought her face would split with the effort.

Lucas stopped so suddenly at the entrance to the room that Hank, following closely behind, almost ran into him. He carried in his left hand a pail of fresh milk.

Lucas grumbled, "I saw the smoke from the chimney, and I supposed you must have lit the fire and gone back to bed."

She was feeding the baby a few bites of soft eggs. She had glasses half full of water in front of both children and broken pieces of biscuits on their plates for them to put in their mouths with their own hands. Nicholas was busy eating his eggs with a spoon and his fingers. He pointed at his new mother, "Lizbeth, Daddy. Ummmm, good."

She lifted the spoon with another tiny bite of eggs and the girl opened her mouth like a bird to receive it.

Lucas placed the pail of milk on the table, then taking a clean jar from the shelf, proceeded to strain the milk through cheesecloth to separate the cream. When he finished, he poured some milk into a couple of small glasses and set them in front of his children and put the remaining liquid in the ice box. Finished with his daily task, he found a chair and sat down. As he crossed behind her, Elizabeth caught a whiff of stale sweat and horse manure, and supposed he'd been up for a long time working in the barn. She glanced down at his boots to keep from showing any expression on her face.

"I always sit here, woman." He glanced at her, and when she stared back, he dropped his eyes.

His face was rumpled with irritation, although Elizabeth was sure she saw grudging admiration in his eyes.

He'd better show her some gratitude, she thought, or he'd have hot coffee in his lap.

She smiled and offered another bite to the girl's mouth, but Priscilla ducked her head back and lifted her arms for her father to pick her up. He ignored the baby. She said something to Prissy and went to the stove for the coffee pot. She filled the cup in front of him and the one in front of the plate where she assumed Hank would sit. She placed all the dishes on the table for them to transfer the food to their own plates and returned to the baby girl. The baby waved her hands in the air and gurgled. Elizabeth gave her a sip of water.

"Will you look at that?" It was the man, Hank Mitchell, staring at the scene in front of him. "Your boy I can play with and dress, Luke, but the baby is a mystery to me. That woman's got magic fingers with that little tyke." He sat at his regular place and took a sip of coffee. He agreed with Nicholas, ummm. He filled his plate with the bacon, potatoes and eggs, and dug in. He looked up, his mouth full, "This is good, ma'am." He rolled his eyes and swallowed.

Lucas also took a sip of coffee and hissed, "Better than what I would'a done myself, Hank, although a little weak for my taste, but I'm not saying anything about that the first morning she's here."

Hank grunted a reply, but Elizabeth didn't hear it. She supposed they were so accustomed to being alone, they didn't consider that she could hear them. Her eyes narrowed before she could catch herself, and she took a deep breath to calm her nerves before turning to the baby once again. The boy watched her every move. She offered him a sip of milk, and he took a long drink, the white liquid dribbling down his chin. She took the napkin and wiped him clean.

Lucas filled his plate and began to eat. He broke open one of the biscuits and knifed some fresh butter and marmalade on it. The two men said nothing for a while, watching the woman pass from the stove to the table, paying attention to the boy and the girl equally and anticipating their every need. They soon started talking about the chores and weather, and Elizabeth listened but didn't interrupt.

"As soon as you finish eating, you can ride the fence line, before the cattle discover a hole and cross over to the Simmons' place. I told Fred last week that he needed to mend his wiring, and he said he'd get to it, but I guess we'll have to do it ourselves. I'll bring some wire and the hammers in the wagon, and we'll see what can be done about it. I want to see about the mare. She don't seem to be carrying this foal well. I sure hope we don't lose her. She's a good breeder."

"I'll check the water in the trough down by the live oaks while I'm riding around. I thought I saw some animal tracks yesterday that don't belong there."

"Wolves, you think?" Lucas frowned at Hank and reached for another biscuit.

"No, more like dogs. I wus talking to Graham in town while I wus waitin' for the stage, and he said a pack of loose dogs wus over to his place last week. Sometimes, dogs is worse than wolves. I'll see if the tracks lead toward the cattle pens on the south range. I'll take my shotgun with me in case I need it."

"Okay, you do that, but don't go chasing off after the dogs and neglect the fence line." Lucas took a last sip of coffee and watched his children eat.

Elizabeth left the children playing with the pieces of biscuit on their plates, took a place at the table and ate while the men talked. She opened a biscuit and spread butter on it. The taste was pleasing to her tongue, light and fluffy with a touch of baking soda. She took a few bites of egg, ate a piece of bacon and returned her attention to

Nicholas. He was becoming restless, kicking his feet against the chair. She wiped his face and hands and let him leave the table on his fat legs and go to the corner to play with his toys.

She finished her own meal and would have enjoyed another cup of coffee, but when she lifted the pot, it was empty. She kept the girl in her chair so she could watch her better. She poured some hot water from the kettle and some cold from the pump and began to wash the dishes and pans she had used to cook breakfast. Hank finished and left for the outdoor chores.

Lucas rose from the table, picked up his son and tossed him in the air. "Don't fall, Boy!"

The boy screamed out in pleasure. "Again, Daddy! Higher!"

Lucas tossed him in the air again and put him on his feet. They played a short game of tag, and Lucas told him to play with his toys. He took the girl from her chair and put his nose in her neck. He took a deep breath, and Elizabeth wondered if he smelled the sweet scent of talcum that she'd spread on her body when she'd bathed and dressed her.

Lucas carried Prissy to the children's bedroom and got her comb and brush. He came back to the kitchen where it was warm and sat on the floor to brush her tangled blond hair. She had brown eyes, and Elizabeth imagined that she must resemble her mother. The boy had brown hair and blue eyes, a combination of mother and father, she supposed. He played with the children for about an hour and rose to join Hank with the chores. He told Elizabeth to find a place for her things and unpack the trunk.

After the men left, Elizabeth finished the dishes and went to the luggage. She opened boxes and tins and put them in what she assumed would be the proper place. She saved most of the toys to give to the children for their birthdays or Christmas, giving them one each from their aunt Wilhelmina: a painted wooden train with an engine, caboose and two cars, pulled by a string for the boy; and a doll, with a china head, arms and legs, with a cloth body for the girl. She was much too young to play with it yet, but she could hold it in her arms. The dress was black and red satin, with tiny ruffles and lace, too nice for sticky little girl fingers, so Elizabeth was determined to make it a wardrobe more suitable for a thirteen-month-old girl. Once the trunk was empty, except for the toys to be saved until later, Elizabeth shoved it against a wall in the living room and covered it with a blanket.

Some of the boxes and tins were for the kitchen, and she was glad to see them. There were multiple lengths of cloth, a jar of mixed buttons, and pins and needles. It made her think of Jed, the drummer, who had ridden the stagecoach with her. She would like to have a really good pair of scissors and a tape measure for the window curtains and table cloth she planned to sew. There were store bought clothes for the children and for Lucas, and new shoes and boots. She hung the clothes in the wardrobes and put the shoes on the shelf.

Her own clothes didn't amount to much; she had four dresses for work days, and one nice dress for church or parties, besides the one she had traveled in to Montana. She had two pairs of shoes and a pair of high-topped button boots for tramping in the woods or farmyard. Wilhelmina had insisted that she would need them. Elizabeth generally wore soft flannel shoes in the house.

*****

At lunchtime, Elizabeth fed the children, bundled them warmly and went outside for some play time. She lay a quilt on the soft grass and let them romp in the yard while she watched them. The dog, Joey, sniffed around the edge of the quilt, hoping for food. When he didn't find any, he lay on the grass, watching the children. The girl crawled to the edge of the quilt, and Elizabeth brought her back until it became a game. Prissy would crook her little face around to see if Elizabeth was watching, then crawl away. Her new mother would grab her dress tail and haul her back. Nicholas ran with his new train, but it ended up lying on the side more often than on its wheels. Elizabeth told him to walk more slowly, but soon he would run again. She decided he needed a flatter surface for the toy.

It was her first chance to really look at the house and grounds. She was disappointed in what she saw. She could see small signs of neglect everywhere, although she supposed the men simply had more work than they could handle with the cattle and horses. There were small tufts of grass at the fence posts and around the barn and house. Most of the grounds had no grass, just dirt and manure.

There were large trees lining the road from town, standing tall and majestic against the sky. She wasn't familiar with the different species, but could tell that some were oaks, some sycamores and there were scrubby bushes near the garden area. There was a large barn and corrals which held several horses. Chickens roamed freely in the grass near the barn. A shelter covered a hog pen and what looked like rabbit hutches. She decided to explore the area. She picked up Prissy and carried her and held Nicholas firmly by the hand. Yes, she found it contained rabbits, black and white, and brown. She pointed them out to the children, and made the sounds of all the farmyard animals as she identified them. She didn't see the men nearby, so assumed they must be out in the fields with the cattle.

The boy tugged at her hand, and she opened the door to the outhouse. She saw a spider web in the corner that she hadn't noticed in the darkness the night before. She looked for a reaction from the children but supposed they were used to such creatures sharing the space. She didn't like it and determined to bring a broom the next time and thoroughly clean the inside of the tiny house. Having been raised in the city, she saw no reason to linger among the pungent odor.

As she exited the small building, she took the boy's hand, held the girl in her arms and they wandered around the grounds. Joey hunkered around, his big head held low. He seemed used to being ignored and was content to follow anyone who was outside. Elizabeth didn't care for his looks, and she turned her head when he was near. The sun was high in the azure sky, but it didn't bring much warmth, and she shivered as she walked. Prissy clung tightly to her neck and she tried to protect her from the chilled wind.

The house itself was built of weathered boards hammered vertically with corner beams of a harder wood. The roof was covered with tin, looked rusted in some areas around the chimney, and slanted toward the porch as if too tired to hold itself up. She looked more closely and noticed a bird's nest in the corner. She wondered if it was recently made or of ancient usage.

The barn was huge compared with the house, the upper story having both a door and window. Elizabeth didn't know much about barns so continued her tramp around the house. There looked to be a former flower bed, grown high with weeds near the east side and edged with tin. She touched her toe to the tin and it fell forward, causing her to quickly step back.

The boy dropped his toy and began to cry.

"It's alright, Nicholas, it's not broken." She stooped, putting the girl on her feet, while she helped him pick up his toy. He broke away and began to run, dragging the toy behind him; she let him run but cautioned him not to go far. The girl remained close to her side, her small hand grasping the tail of Elizabeth's coat.

The multi-bladed windmill creaked and groaned as the wind shifted and the rotor flew into a different direction. The wooden lattice tower looked to be about thirty feet high, and there was a large, galvanized tin container holding the water from the pump cylinder. A metal ladder crawled up one side, reaching to just below the rotor. She hadn't noted that the wind had picked up. She called to the boy, and they returned to the house by the back door. She helped them remove their outer garments and hung them on pegs on the wall.

*****

The rest of the morning was spent becoming familiar with the objects in the house. She had no idea if the men would return for lunch, so she made a simple stew and cornbread. They didn't return. She put the children to scratching with pencils on squares of paper she found in a desk drawer and began to scrub the kitchen from top to bottom. The boy soon became restless, so she gave him a broom and showed him how to brush the dust toward the back door. He wasn't very helpful but found the broom entertaining, and he was soon pretending to ride it through the house, his childish voice mimicking that of his father. She laughed with the sheer pleasure of the sound.

While the children took a short nap, Elizabeth found a small piece of cloth and cut a pattern for a doll dress from a newspaper she found in the kindling box. The scissors she had in her luggage were dull, making it hard to cut, so she looked for another pair in the kitchen. There was a pair of large shears, but no sewing type scissors. She decided to ask Lucas if he had a way to sharpen them. After cutting the cloth, she sat in a chair to sew a simple dress for the china doll, to preserve the red and black satin dress in which it was purchased. With still some stitching to complete, she put the cloth in her sewing basket, and rose to peel potatoes for supper.

The children awoke, and she sat Nicholas at the table with a piece of paper and pencil. She showed him how to make marks with the pencil on the paper, and he quickly grasped the concept, but his fingers weren't trained. She had to frequently stop her cooking to help him. She talked to Prissy, strapped in her special chair with a long piece of cloth, and gave her some spoons to bang on the table. Between the two children, she was kept busy picking up spoons and pencils and paper from the floor, but it was entertaining, and she was patient with them.

The sun had already sunk into the horizon when the men returned to the kitchen. Elizabeth had supper ready to eat, with the table set with dishes and cutlery. Two lamps were lighted and sent their radiance into the corners of the room. Hot coffee was perking on the stove, and a fresh loaf of bread was baking in the oven. There were sliced steaks of fried beef and smooth smashed potatoes, turnips and fried fruit pies for desert. The children had been fed and were playing in the corner away from the stove.

"Ma'am," Hank murmured, pulling his hat respectfully from his head. He nodded. When Lucas stood dumbly, he kicked him with the side of his boot, "Tell her it looks nice."

Elizabeth pressed her lips together and frowned, stricken by the fact that Hank, the hired man, had better manners than her husband. They had no way of knowing how many times she had been forced to fetch and carry and tug the children out of harm's way of the stove. She was exhausted, her hair was damp from sweat and small ringlets fell about her ears. She quickly brushed them back onto her head.

Lucas grunted a type of greeting and put his hat and

coat on the pegs by the door. He greeted the children in the corner of the room, and they clambered for their daddy to stay beside them and play, but he went to the table, placed the milk bucket on it, and commenced to strain the cream from the top. Prissy started on hands and knees to follow him, but Elizabeth took her to the chair and strapped her in with a scarf. Nicholas watched the proceedings with curiosity and went back to his building blocks.

Hank had brought in about a half-dozen eggs and washed them at the sink. Neither spoke again to the woman. With their chores done, and the milk and eggs put away, they sat down at the table. Elizabeth brought the coffee pot and filled their cups. Back and forth, she traveled from stove to table, carrying food and dishes to the men. She carefully kept her eyes on the boy in the corner. She gave the girl an empty bowl and spoon to play with. The men ate and left the room to finish their outdoors chores.

Elizabeth bathed the children one at a time from a basin of warm water and put them to bed, and finally sat to eat her own meal. The food was cold, but it was tasty. She filled the kettle and made herself a soothing cup of tea. She sat for some time, contemplating her situation.

With a sigh of resignation, she washed the dishes and pots and skillet. She wiped the table, swept the floor and looked around at the room. Taking one of the lamps with her, she went to the bedroom, washed herself and again put on the white cotton gown and crawled into bed. She was lonely and discouraged. And, so tired that her eyes closed and she slept. She didn't awaken when the man undressed and moved into the bed beside her.

— 4 —

The next day at the ranch was a repeat of the first, except that Elizabeth decided she couldn't abide the unkempt front room. After settling the children in the kitchen, she picked up the old newspapers, put books back on the shelves, and dusted the furniture. She invited the children into the room and read to them from a book she found on the shelf. It was a tale probably too adult for them to understand, but she persevered until they became restless, and she tickled their ribs and had them rolling on the floor with laughter. They settled down with their toys again while she heated a bucket of water, and using a portion of the lye soap, got on her knees and scrubbed the floor. From there, she moved to the baseboards, then to the trim around the windows. The wallpaper would have to wait until later, as the work took half a day, and there were meals to prepare. She poured the water onto the ground, rinsed her cloths, and cooked a hearty vegetable soup and a cake. She watched the children playing with their toys and put them down for a nap in the afternoon, while she stitched the doll dress.

She couldn't understand why Lucas didn't approach

her in the night, although she knew he slept beside her. Maybe, he was grieving for his first wife, she thought, who had so recently been lost to him. Lucas hadn't looked into her eyes at the table or spoken to her while he and Hank were eating. They had talked to each other about the cattle or horses or fence lines, so she knew it wasn't a matter of required silence at mealtimes. She tried to remember what the priest said about accepting a husband's advances, but what was she to do when he didn't even speak to her in a friendly manner? She was used to many people around, most of them children, for sure, but at least there was talk and laughter and running footsteps. Here, there was silence. A silence that left her puzzled and almost frightened.

On the next day, as soon as the men left the house, she took the children out for some sunshine and exercise. After half an hour, they seemed tired, so she led them onto the back porch, removed their outer garments, and examined the clothes washer at the end of the porch. It had a galvanized steel round tub that had a rotating drum powered by a crank. There was another crank that squeezed the clothes to remove the excess water. She tried both mechanisms until she was satisfied that she could work them in a satisfactory manner. She wondered how she was to get the water into the tubs. She saw no other way, so filled two metal pails with water, heated them on the kitchen range, poured the water into the large washer tub, and set the buckets with more water on the stove for heating again. While they were heating, she sorted the clothes she found in a basket in the hallway. She looked closely at each of the tiny children's clothing for tears or holes, put two pieces aside for mending, did the same with the shirts and denims of her husband, collected her own garments and made piles on the floor of the porch. The children delighted in playing in the garments, while she washed the bed linens in the hot sudsy water. She filled the two big enamel tubs for rinsing the garments, and when each tub full was thoroughly scrubbed, hung them on the clothes line strung from one tree to another. It was a back-breaking chore, but something that must be done. She would remember next time to ask Hank if he needed his clothing washed. While the sun was drying the clothing, she entertained the children with amusing stories of the children at the orphanage, and mended the garments she had held aside. The image of her friend Selena from the orphanage crossed her mind, and she wondered where she was today. Coming out of her short melancholy, she began to prepare the evening meal.

That night, Elizabeth was determined to stay awake, so that she would be ready when her husband came into the bed. But, he didn't climb into bed until very late, and her eyes wouldn't stay open. She awoke to the sound of children's laughter, quickly dressed and followed the sound. Lucas was dressing the children in their bedroom. She decided to join the merriment, grasped Prissy around the arms and lifted her nightgown from her warm, pink body. She took the dress that Lucas had selected and helped her into it. As soon as Nicholas was dressed, Lucas took him into the kitchen where it was warm. He poured water into the coffee pot and placed it on the stove. When Elizabeth entered the room with Prissy, Lucas left for his morning chores.

After two more miserable, lonely nights, there was a change in her husband's behavior. On this night, he crawled into bed beside her, but it was different. He awakened her. He was murmuring strange things, and she lay still as a leaf, waiting to see if he was angry with her or would leave her to sleep alone once again.

"Oh, hell! I can't stand it no more." His words were low in tone, and they tore at the curtain of darkness in the room. "Willie was right. I'm overwhelmed with lust for a stranger."

Elizabeth listened with surprise. He seemed to be talking to himself. Recently, she had dreamed that one of the children at the orphanage had burned an arm at the stove. She felt the man's arm around her, and it somehow reminded her of the dream. It was dark, and she could barely make out his form. Her heart rhythm increased. She tried to make her breathing steady.

"I'm a man, and I can no longer lie beside you without wanting you. Your hair smells so clean, and you're warm when I draw near like this. How I wish you were awake to answer my sincerest entreaties." Her heart was softened. She'd seen him caressing a ceramic figurine of a dancing couple that had been his wife's. He must feel he was being unfaithful. She felt him lean to her, and she didn't speak. She pulled him closer and let the events of the night teach her of the mysteries of the marriage bed.

*****

Elizabeth awoke before dawn alone in the bed, but it wasn't as before. She reached over and pulled his pillow to her. She breathed deeply of the intoxicating scent of his hair and shaving soap. Her man, she thought, he was her man. All the gossip and stories she'd heard at the orphanage didn't begin to reveal the glory of being a woman with her own man. She roused herself when she heard a sound from the children's room. Quickly, she washed, dressed in a clean dress and left her hair streaming down in back. She didn't have time to braid it. She went to the children, and her day began as it had for the days she'd been in her husband's home, but this morning she felt exhausted but deeply satisfied.

— 5 —

On Saturday night, the men came in later than usual and smelled of horse and cattle. Elizabeth stood at the stove stirring the beans, and she was startled when Lucas came from behind and encircled her with his arms. She yelped in shock, and the children began to clamor for attention.

"Tomorrow's Sunday, and we get up early for the worship service. I don't hold much for religious notions, but I promised my wife I'd teach the children the Bible and attend the meeting. Put on that dress you wore on the train; I kinda liked that color. And, have the children clean and ready before seven, so we'll have time to arrive before the singing starts."

"Ah, Lucas," Hank called, interrupting. "Can you see fit to give me a few bucks. I'm going to ride into town tonight."

Lucas turned away from the stove and looked at Hank. "You're not going to church with us?"

"Ah, you know I like a different kind of entertainment on a weekend." He hefted his hat onto the back of his head and stood awkwardly near the door.

Lucas turned to pick a lard can from a top shelf. He opened it and took out a few paper bills, and without looking to see the amount, handed them to his friend. "Hank, you don't have to ask every time you want a little cash. What I have, you're welcome to. I've told you that many times."

"I know, Boss. But it don't seem proper for me to just take it without your knowing about it. Thanks. I'll be on my way, then, 'Night, Elizabeth. 'Night, children." And he was gone from the house before Elizabeth could acknowledge his disappearance.

She put the remaining dishes on the table and was struck by the silence. The boy was looking down at his plate, and Prissy was gazing at her father. Lucas sat down and began to fill his son's plate with food. The food was passed, the forks and spoons were lifted, and for the first time since her arrival, Elizabeth wasn't sure what to say.

The children were put to bed early, after she gave them a bath. Lucas had retreated to some unknown place outside, and she finished the dishes, turned the lamp low and went to bed. She heard Lucas come in and the sound of his bathing. He came to bed slightly damp and undressed. She drew him gratefully into her arms and heard the lonesome sound of a cow mooing in the distance. A faint gleam of light shown through the crack of the window shade, and the creak of the bedsprings was the only sound heard in the night.

Before the dawn, Lucas was in the barn, milking the cow, and throwing some hay to the horses. He hitched the horse to the wagon and helped the children, spotless in their new clothing, into the seat. Joey ran around, interested in this change in routine, and he barked at the children in their fine things. Lucas shooed him away before he climbed in with Prissy and Nicholas. Elizabeth climbed in beside them, dressed as he had asked her, and he drove toward town. Joey followed for a time before turning around and heading back up the road. It was a beautiful morning, the sky was softly pink on the horizon and the air smelled fresh and clean. After a while, Lucas began to whistle, and the children joined in with their childish chatter.

He drove into the church yard, and Elizabeth could see a line of wagons near the building. It was a large, white building with a tall steeple. The bell was tolling the call to worship. She sat straighter in the seat, wondering what the people would think of her. When Lucas stopped the horse under the shade of a tree, she saw a few women standing near the door, gawking at them. A couple of men started toward the wagon. She quickly climbed down and lifted the children down from the side.

"Heh, Lucas, we wondered if you'd make it to town today. I saw Hank at the Green Grass Parlor, and he seemed to be having a good time." A bear of a man in a high, stiff collar laughed and clapped Lucas on the back as he finished tending to the team. "Name's Caldwell, Mrs. Thompson. I live over on Rattlesnake Slough, run the Flying C spread."

"I don't guess we'll see you there no more, now you got yourself another wife. Is this her? Hank said she was a good cook. I might come around some time and see for myself." A tall, slightly stooped man with a full beard and mustache bowed to Elizabeth.

"Frank Slaughter, Elizabeth. You haven't met him." Lucas introduced the tall, slender man.

"How-do, ma'am," a man dressed in the overalls and blue-plaid shirt of a farmer said. "Don't you mind our teasing none. I heard about this proxy marriage stuff, and I just might be tempted to git my own wife, only I been a bachelor so long, I don't rightly know if a woman would have me." He laughed, and the other men laughed with him.

"We best be getting to the door, men, or the singing will start without us. That's the only reason why I come here on a Sunday. Can you sing, Mrs. Thompson? I'll tell my wife to ask you to join the choir, if you can." A short, bald man had come up and tried to move the group toward the white building. Elizabeth could hear the faint sound of a piano and a violin playing.

"Darling, this is Clay Bennett, the town mayor, and you just met that tall gangly fellow. He's our neighbor on the south, Frank Slaughter." Lucas had the small hand of his son in one hand and took Prissy up onto his shoulders, leaving Elizabeth to welcome the men as they strolled toward the door.

One woman came forward. As soon as she arrived, she took Prissy from his shoulders and sat her on her feet.

"Good morning, Lucas. I'll take the children to the classroom, so they can play with the other children. Hello, Mrs. Thompson. I'm Mattie Breedlove, on Sunday, the younger children's nursemaid and teacher. I'm glad to meet you."

"Thank you, ma'am." Elizabeth watched as the woman led the children to a side door and disappeared with the children. She felt bereft without them. She turned to the other women, but they walked into the church, the men following behind.

It was cool and dim inside the building, with the only light filtering from the stained glass window high in the wall behind the alter and piano and a few lanterns and candles strategically placed here and there. A very thin, white haired man was playing the violin, standing beside a large woman dressed in a blue gingham dress with an enormous matching hat on her head that tilted back and forth as she pounded on the keys of the instrument. What she lacked in talent, she made up in energy.

There were maybe two dozen people sitting scattered

among the pews, and a family with several children was near the front. Elizabeth had time to wonder why the children didn't attend the class with the teacher, but she was distracted by the whispers going on between two older women, one leaning over the back of a pew talking to her neighbor behind.

"There she is, Sue, his new wife. I heard his sister picked her up in an orphanage."

"Shhh, Betty, she'll hear you."

"I don't care. I heard tell that he never set eyes on her until she came on the stage. She don't have a family at all, Hank said."

Lucas guided Elizabeth into a pew a few feet ahead and they could no longer hear the woman's loud whisper. He placed his hat on the seat beside him, and Elizabeth could see that his hair was untidy. He must have read her thoughts, for he reached up and smoothed it down. She saw a book in the rack in front of them, and he reached for it. A shuffle of feet was heard, and she turned to look toward the back.

A large woman wearing purple from the top of her head to the floor was striding up the aisle, leaving a puff of perfume behind that made Elizabeth slightly nauseous. She was hanging on the arm of an enormous man dressed in a black suit. She nodded to the right and left as she passed them to sit on the second pew from the front. She then turned to look over the crowd while the man retreated back down the aisle to sit in the last row by the door. Elizabeth wanted to squirm as she saw the woman's eyes fall on her. She remembered her manners from the orphanage and smiled shyly at the woman before she turned her back on the congregation.

The music stopped, and she felt Lucas shift his position, as though he were uncomfortable, or embarrassed. From the side door, a short, squat man came through wearing the vestments of a minister, and he sat in the lone chair at the front. He was followed by the choir, only six people, singing slightly off key as they tried to find their places in the chairs provided. Elizabeth watched the purple hat dip as though in acknowledgment of the start of the service. The audience rose, and the music continued.

The preacher seemed to go on and on, and Elizabeth wished she had the children with her. She hadn't attended many worship services and wasn't familiar with the words of the hymns or the prayers. But, at last, it ended, and the people began to move down the aisle to the outside, where they stood in groups, chattering. A young lady brought the children to Lucas, and he took Prissy in his arms. Nicholas clung to Elizabeth's hand, and she stooped to welcome him with a kiss on the cheek. The other children ran about the yard in abandonment, around the trees and the wagons, as though freedom was something cherished. She caught a whiff of the strong perfume and turned as the woman in purple approached.

"Lucas, you will introduce me to your new wife, if you please." She gave Elizabeth a glare through her horn-rimmed glasses.

"Permilla, this is Elizabeth, who has come from Chicago."

The lady nodded and reached out her purple-gloved hand. Elizabeth took it and gave it a slight shake. She remembered all the gentlemen and ladies in the drawing room of the orphanage and smiled with a shy murmur of greeting. Surprisingly, the woman smiled back, showing a full set of white teeth. There was a small mole near her right eye. She was heavily powdered and rouged, and Elizabeth could see the heavy wrinkles of age under the paint.

"Do you speak, Child?" She looked at Lucas as if he'd made a mistake, and this couldn't be the woman he'd chosen to marry.

"Yes, Permilla. She speaks." He smiled and nodded to Elizabeth. "Well, Wife? Speak up."

"Pleased," Elizabeth choked out, feeling very out of place in the woman's presence.

"Thank God for that." She inclined her head towards Elizabeth as if dismissing her and turned to Lucas. "Your children have a nanny, now, at least. I'm sure she can't educate them, but that won't matter much, you being on that ranch. They'll have a chance to attend a regular school when they're older. Have you replaced your carriage? Four will be using it, now. You can't expect your children to crowd in with you and your new wife."

"We're fine, Permilla. I assure you." He seemed amused by her comment. He leaned in to Elizabeth and whispered, "You can speak your mind, you know. You're my wife, now."

She couldn't, however. Her memories of the orphanage were too strong. She forced herself to occasionally murmur a response and was surprised when a younger man entered into the conversation.

"This is the bride, I see. She's so very different from Margaret." He smiled and bowed to Elizabeth, and she could smell the liquor on his breath.

"So people tell me." She found a bit of courage, remembering her first night when Lucas had questioned her virginity. "Is that a bad thing?"

"Oh, dear," Permilla squawked, putting her hand to her mouth. "Lucas!"

"I told you she speaks. Introduce your son-in-law to my wife, Permilla. It's the polite thing to do."

Elizabeth recognized him as the man who'd escorted the woman up the aisle, and now she understood why. Permilla smiled warmly for the first time, said she liked outspoken women, introduced him as Todd Wellington, told them to have a good day, frowned at the children clinging to Lucas's hands and walked away to speak to the other people, with her son-in-law on her arm.

"Come, we can go now. You've won her over, you know. If she approves of you, the others will, too." He walked to the wagon, tossed the children into the back with a fatherly pinch and a giggle, and helped Elizabeth onto the passenger seat. He stood for a moment in silence. "She didn't like Margaret." He sighed and went to loosen the horse's reins. He was silent as he drove away from the church as if in deep thought.

After riding for a while, Elizabeth asked, "Todd compared me to Margaret. Is that why she likes me, because I'm different?"

"Possibly. In fact, I think it's the very reason." He smiled. "You're very different. I'm beginning to understand what a good thing that is."

"Why is Permilla's opinion so important? Who'd pay attention to a woman? She must be very rich."

"She's the widow of the largest rancher in the district. Her parents were the first pioneers in the county, and she married the man, folks say, out of spite, because they brought a man from the East for her husband and she didn't like him. Her father is said to have been a very dominant and cruel character, but I suppose a man had to be to survive in the early days, when the land was wild, and the Indians untamed. Casper was half Sioux, and they ran off and married without permission. It was a big scandal of its day, long before my time. They lived on the Sioux reservation and had two children. When her father died, she returned to the ranch, and her husband ran it until his death. The man with her is the foreman and her son-in-law." The horse trotted slowly up the road, and he seemed to have finished his history lesson, but Elizabeth wasn't satisfied.

"Where's the daughter? Is she still alive?"

"No, she drowned in a sudden flood of the river. They

were crossing the stream, and she was thrown into the water. The body was never found. The wagon was caught in some debris, and the horse's body was washed down the river several miles. They had no children."

"That's sad. She has no family besides her son-in-law?"

"Besides young Tom Wellington? Her son's alive. He and his wife live in Helena and have several children. He's well-educated and into politics. I suppose the ranch'll be sold someday if none of the grandchildren want to live there."

He drove into the yard, and Elizabeth saw Hank sitting in the shade of the barn, a leather harness in his hand. He rose and threw the harness carelessly on the ground when they approached and came to the head of the horse. He was wearing his usual work clothes.

"Heh, Boss. I wus waiting for you. I saw some tracks near the stock tank in the south pasture. Looks like a cougar or other big cat. The animals didn't seem disturbed, so I came back to the house. Sure was a roaring time in town last night at the Green Grass Parlor. Clancy and Felden from the Bar H had quite a fight, afore the sheriff broke it off. Melody was asking for you." While he was talking, Elizabeth and Lucas helped the children from the wagon, and they headed for the rope swing under the tree. She thought of calling them back before they got their clothes dirty, but she was more interested in the conversation.

"What is the Green Grass Parlor, a saloon?" She squinted up at the men, the sun shining in her eyes.

"Uh, shouldn't have mentioned that, Boss."

"It's okay, Hank. She'll find out soon enough, anyway. It's the local bordello, a gentlemen's club, with drinking, gambling and women."

"I see." She turned to Hank. "Were the men injured from their fighting?"

"Nah, just a few bruises and cuts. They've already gone back to the ranch."

"Where's the Bar H? Is it far from here?" As she spoke, she noticed that Nicholas had stopped pushing Prissy on the swing, and they seemed to be having a fight of their own started. She began to move to them, and Lucas followed. Hank remained by the wagon and climbed aboard to put it in the shed and unhitch the horse.

"It's Madame Chatwin's place," Lucas shared, as they walked. "About fifteen miles to the north along the county road. Nicholas, stop antagonizing your sister. It's time you went into the house." Prissy clambered down from the swing with her brother's help, and the children ran ahead to the house. "Elizabeth, stop a minute." He gazed at Hank, busy by the barn. He kept his eyes focused on him as he confessed.

"I'm not a saint, dear. Before you came, I was lonely and grieving. The Green Grass Parlor helped pass the time. Melody Trent is a good listener and beautiful. I spent a lot of time with her. But, you needn't worry about her. That's all over. I told her I was getting married. She accepted it." He started walking again, with a glance at her troubled face.

Elizabeth said not a word. She walked into the house and helped the children with their clothes, and started the noon meal. After they had eaten, the men left on horses, and she put the leftover food away, cold. When he came to her bed in the dark, she didn't turn him away, although her heart was heavy with doubt and jealousy. His wife was dead, and she could cope with her ghost, but Melody Trent was alive and available.

— 6 —

The days turned to weeks and seemed long and dreary, with no neighbors coming to visit. Her only time away from the ranch was on Sunday, and she was grateful to have other women with whom to talk. They seemed to forget that hers had been a proxy marriage and shared favorite recipes and helpful hints on how to raise children. The children were cheerful, and Elizabeth spent most of her time with them. She took them on nature walks to the creek and pointed out birds, squirrels, or the cows and horses in the field. Joey often accompanied them, and she grew attached to his presence, although she rarely gave him more than a quick pat on the head. Prissy surprised her Daddy one night when she grabbed his leg and began to moo like a cow. He was thrilled and threw her into the air to hear her squeal. Elizabeth saw him smile at odd times. Once he was working on the corral, and as she looked out the window, he suddenly stopped and looked into the distance as if seeing a colorful rainbow on a clear day. Another time he was shoeing a horse, and she learned he'd dropped the hammer and had run to the house during one of the children's naps. Hank remarked when he found Lucas in the house with Elizabeth, "That's very odd behavior." He scratched his head in puzzlement, before heading outside to pick up the hammer and finish the job left undone.

Only one event occurred to mar the pleasant atmosphere that had developed at the ranch since Elizabeth's arrival. After an uneventful week that had become almost ordinary, of breakfast with the children, lunches either at the kitchen table or alongside the creek, and afternoons of playtime, cleaning, or preparing Lucas's evening meal, Elizabeth had collected the washing from the basket in the hallway and dumped the various items in the kitchen floor. Prissy was given the task of sorting the colors from one pile into another, but she soon lost interest and fell asleep on the towels with the doll that Wilhelmina had sent in her hand. After about an hour running the clothes through the washer on the back porch, she carried a reed basket to the yard to hang the items to dry. As she laid a pair of boy's trousers over the line and reached into her apron for a clothespin, the dog began barking frantically. She glanced toward the sound and felt her heart jump into her throat. Nicholas hung on the ladder of the windmill tower, his short legs barely able to move from step to step, pulling himself ever higher.

"Nicholas!" She choked off her word, afraid she'd startle him. She glanced at the house. She had to trust that Prissy was still asleep. Pulling the bib of her apron over her head, she dropped it with its pouch of clothespins into the basket and jogged towards the towering windmill. She shushed the dog, saying, "Quiet, Joey. Hush, now." Looking up, she shaded her eyes from the sun with one hand. As the blades turned, the sun flashed repeatedly across her face, the intermittent shadows seeming like a forewarning of disaster. Her heart pounded. She didn't want to frighten the boy and make him fall.

"Honey, what are you doing?" she called in an even

tone. He stopped climbing and looked at her, and he smiled. Her throat tightened, and she prayed for him to hold on with both hands.

"I'm climbing, 'Lizbeth. See? I'm almost to the top." He looked up and reached his hand to the next rung.

"You did climb high. Can you stay right there?" Oh, God, she thought. What if he falls? How could I have not watched him better? "Elizabeth wants you to come down, please."

"I will, just not yet." He'd worked himself one step higher, and his hands were white with holding on. The blades rattled, and in a gust of wind, they spun with increasing intensity. "I'm scared, 'Lizbeth. I want down."

"Okay, Baby. Stay right there." Elizabeth dreaded climbing the tower. She'd never been one for high places. She grabbed her skirt and tied the side into a fat knot to free up her legs, and she placed one hand on the ladder. "I'll be right there, Nicholas. Hold on tight."

"I will. Please hurry." The blades shook the tower, and he began to cry.

By the time Elizabeth had him in her arms, she was also crying, whether from fright or relief, she wasn't about to admit. She slowly descended the ladder, step by cautious step, the boy clinging to her neck. Reaching the ground, she released him to walk on his own. Lucas—oddly prescient Lucas—managed to arrive just as she turned the boy loose. She stood to see his eyes take in the unfinished laundry, with the boy's trousers hanging, one leg flopping loosely, and Nicholas jumping up and down in excitement over his adventure. Before Elizabeth could explain, Lucas erupted.

"What is this?" He ran, swooped the boy into his arms and began looking him over. When he saw no injuries, he glared at Elizabeth. "I saw someone on the tower, but I had no idea it was the boy. How could you ... if he'd fallen . . ." He crushed the boy to him.

"I'm so sorry," she began. "The baby was asleep, and I was hanging clothes. I didn't realize he was up there, until Joey barked. It won't happen again, I promise."

Lucas took several deep breaths and let the final one out in a long sigh, finally saying, "No one's injured. Thank God for that. You've got to be responsible, Elizabeth. I can't hover over the children because you're doing laundry. You've got to do both. Is that clear?"

"Yes. I can do this." Elizabeth glanced at her skirt and the knot still there, then she looked away.

"Make sure you do," he said. "Where's Prissy?"

"In the house, asleep." She looked at him to find his attention on the boy.

"Come, Nicholas, we're heading to the house to see about your sister."

Elizabeth watched them walk away with dismay, and not wanting to be with Lucas inside, she untied her skirt, returned to her basket and dutifully began to hang the rest of her washing to dry.

Jed Masters, the drummer, came by twice on his rounds to the farms and ranches. Elizabeth was pleased to find that he had two pairs of scissors in his pack and she chose the larger pair. She also bought a meat grinder and a dozen cannery jars with lids. Jed was overheard to say to a ranch hand at the Bar H about the change in Lucas Thompson since his proxy wife had arrived. No longer the brooding, lonely man, Lucas laughed and told a few racy jokes while in town buying chicken feed at the local market. The lines on his craggy face softened, and a deep contentment was in his voice. He often took his son riding on the front of his saddle and played with the children on Sunday afternoons. Jed confided to the neighbor that he might find himself a wife in the same way and had written to a matrimonial agency in Chicago. He had expectations of a woman arriving soon. The wife quickly spread the juicy gossip to her friends.

Elizabeth knitted warm mittens and socks for Hank and Lucas, but she had a special surprise for her husband, although she thought he already knew it. There was no other reason for him to be at the house as often as he had. Why else would he show up and ask her how she was doing?

One day Elizabeth stepped into the barn to fetch some apples from the barrel, and overheard the men talking. Joey was asleep at the door, and he opened his eyes and looked at her. She held her finger to her lips and started to back out, but Hank's deep voice drew her attention.

"What's gotten into you, Boss? You're acting like a lovesick bull. I hardly know you anymore, leaving the chores undone and going up to the house at odd times." Hank's voice had a tone that Elizabeth hadn't heard before. He sounded almost angry.

"It's Elizabeth, Hank, I'm worried about her. She hasn't had a menses period since she arrived, and that was three months ago. It must have happened that first night, I figure. I didn't expect more children so soon. I hoped Nicky and Prissy could enjoy their childhood years."

"Is that all that's troubling you? It stands to reason, Luke, that a man like you and a woman like Elizabeth would have children soon after marriage. The little tyke will be company for the children. I'm glad for you, old boy."

Elizabeth quickly withdrew from the barn without the apples she had sought. She thought she'd heard a note of exasperation in her husband's voice, but she thought he sounded pleased, too. She later became agitated when she realized that he'd spoken more freely than she'd have liked, but the men had been friends for years, so she dismissed it from her mind, forgotten with the upcoming preparations for the Christmas season. With the cold weather and the occasional snow, the children were difficult to manage, and she had her hands full with her chores.

The smell of roasting Christmas turkey and apple pie made the whole house seem festive. Elizabeth took the toys that Wilhelmina had sent in September for the children, wrapped them in brown paper and tied the presents with twine. She wrapped the mittens for Hank in an old newspaper. Hank had captured the wild turkey in a trap in the forest above the ranch. He didn't like to shoot the birds because he claimed the buckshot made the creatures taste bad. Lucas chopped down a small tree, and it stood in the parlor ready to be decorated with ribbons, candles, and tiny bells he had found in the mercantile store at Billings when he went to sell a bull.

The day before Christmas, the family gathered in the parlor and decorated the tree while the children stood watching in amazement. They clapped their hands in imitation of their father, mother and Hank.

"Would you look at that? I haven't seen a sight like that since I left home." Hank's face was red, for the candles glowed with a radiance that awakened long forgotten memories in the hired hand. He took out his kerchief and blew his nose. Nicky went to him and pulled on his trousers' leg.

"Hank, up! So I can see the angel on top!" Hank put the boy on his shoulders so he could see the highest bough. "Look, 'Lisbeth. The angel has wings." The boy clung to Hank's thick mop of hair to steady himself. He turned so he could see his mother and father. "Look, Prissy!" He reached to touch the flame of a candle, but Hank drew him back and put him on his feet.

Lucas put the last red shiny ball on the tree and picked up Prissy so she could see the angel. He'd just turned to bring his wife closer, when she grimaced and started collecting the wrapping paper and put away the boxes.

Elizabeth looked at her family with sadness in her heart. She hadn't known the pleasure of a family Christmas before. All the children at the orphanage got one gift from the matron, and some peppermint sticks and cherry ball candy, and an orange and an apple. She had no candy or oranges to give to the children, but she had nuts and apples. She forced a smile on her face when she saw the look in her husband's eyes.

She and Lucas put the children to bed after Hank left for his own cabin and sat on the sofa admiring the twinkling flames from the lit candles. He turned to her and said, "I know your secret, Elizabeth. I'm very glad. It'll be a boy, I know, for I need another worker on the ranch."

She laughed. They blew out the candles and retreated to the bedroom.

*****

In late January, Elizabeth felt a sharp pain in her side and she knew that the baby was in trouble. It was a cold day, and sleet and snow had fallen the night before. Icicles hung from the tree branches and the roofs of the house and barn. She rang the bell on the back porch for emergencies, shivering in the cold wind. With great care, she took the children to their room for safety, told them to play quietly with their toys, before she removed her dress and crawled in bed, the pain so bad that she wanted to scream. She gritted her teeth and endured, for she didn't want to alarm the children.

Hank heard the bell first and ran to the house. He guessed what happened, because he fled to the corral and sped off on his favorite stallion for town and the midwife. Lucas came a few minutes later from the pond where he was cracking the ice for the cattle to drink. He raced into the kitchen, but no one was there. He heard the children's laughter in their room and assured them that he was there with them. He moved into the room he shared with Elizabeth and found her curled in a hard knot of pain, trying not to call out and scare the children. He noticed a damp spot on the floor and saw blood. He went to the bed and told her he was there with her, then went to the kitchen and put water on the stove to boil.

Three hours later, Hank took the tiny, misshapen body of a boy, wrapped him in a towel and buried him by a stone outcropping on the hill. He found a twig from a nearby tree and marked the spot, but could do nothing more until the weather cleared. He knelt and said a prayer for the little mite who hadn't had a chance to live.

The midwife worked frantically to save Elizabeth, who was bleeding profusely. She was pale and wan, her face drawn with pain. Lucas watched over the children, nervous and fidgety. He put the children to bed and sat in the kitchen throughout the night, praying for forgiveness and promising God to obey him in all things, if he would save his wife from the pain she was enduring. At last, around three of the morning, the bleeding stopped, and clots formed in her womb. By four, she was sleeping soundly and breathing naturally.

The midwife came out of the room wiping her hands on a cloth. "Your woman will be fine, with rest and good food." Without further words, she stepped to the sink and began to scrub her hands.

"Will . . . will she be able to have . . ." Lucas dropped his head, and wiped his eyes.

"Children?" the midwife called over her shoulder. "I should think so. She's young and strong. I'm leaving some laudanum; if the pain increases, you call the doctor. The medicine'll help her sleep while her body heals."

Before Lucas could thank her, she was gone, her buggy crunching over the frozen ground back to her home.

"Luke, boy, you be okay?" Hank turned his hat in his hands, worrying the brim. "I'll be on my way, now. I'll say a prayer for the missus, and for you, too. Health for her, and that you don't feel no guilt over something that's not your fault. There's nothing you could have done to prevent this. That woman has brought you nothing but joy, and you know it."

"You finished, Hank? I don't feel like any company tonight. Go to bed, please." He didn't look up as his friend left the house.

Lucas sat in the kitchen all night. He rose several times to check on his wife and children, and went back to his meditation. His craggy face was pale and haggard. His eyes grew red-rimmed from tears not shed. Just before dawn, he sat with his arms on his legs and his hands over the back of his head, and he whispered, "God, 'twas your will that the boy not live. It was nothing to do with either me or my wife." With those few words, he rose, rebuilt the fire in the stove and began to cook chicken broth for Elizabeth and flapjacks for the children. He sliced large slabs of ham and fried them to perfection. He made porridge for himself and Hank.

By the time Elizabeth awoke, tired and sad, Lucas had a strong grip on his emotions. "Are you able to rise?" He stepped to the bedside and stroked her face.

"If I don't get up, this bed won't be fit to lie in. Help me outside, Lucas, I've got to relieve myself, even if it pains me to do so. Help me up, Husband."

He helped her to the outhouse, his arm across her back, one painful step at a time. Joey followed them, whining, as if he knew something bad had happened. Back in the house, Lucas helped her back to the bed. He put fresh, clean sheets on the bed. As he was adjusting the pillows at her back, Elizabeth started to cry.

"How, Lucas? Why?"

"It's God's will. No one can know why, Sweetheart."

"Where is he? It was a boy? Please tell me God gave us a boy." She pressed her fist to her mouth, trying to stop the sobs that racked her body.

"Yes, a boy. God sent us a boy; but then He took him back to live with Him. I'm sorry, Elizabeth. Hank took him to the hill, up by the stone outcrop. I'll put a cross there when the weather turns."

"A cross on the hill." She shivered, and with a final sob of pain gathered herself. "Where are the children, Lucas? Are the children alright?"

"They're asleep. I fed them and gave them some picture books, and Nicky talked to Prissy. They fell asleep on the floor, so I left them there, covered with a blanket. I'll put them in the bed when you've eaten."

"Daniel. That's his name: Daniel Lee."

"What?"

"On the cross; put the name Daniel Lee Thompson. I like that name; it's strong and brave."

Lucas gave her a smile. With patience and tender touches, he served her the chicken broth to help her regain her strength. She went to sleep, and he helped her lie back among the sheets. She was in bed for eight days, until the doctor determined it was safe for her to return to her duties.

Lucas left the majority of the chores to Hank, while he stayed with Elizabeth and the children, so that she wouldn't be tempted to lift Prissy and harm herself. It was a strain on the household, for the two small children clambered for her attention even more than Lucas.

— 7 —

Elizabeth slowly regained her strength and was back to normal by mid-February. She prepared breakfast for the children, read to Nicholas for a short time each day and showed Prissy she could make a doll from a corn husk. The girl loved it so, she made a whole family. They didn't last, though. The dog ran in as the door was opened one day and tore them apart. Prissy cried, but she was soon over it.

As painful as her ordeal and grief had been, Elizabeth noticed that Lucas and Hank worked hard during that harsh winter, with snow in drifts as high as the house roof. She'd never seen so much snow. Despite their best efforts, several cattle died and lay stiff and cold on the ground. One of the mares was tangled in the fence and had to be shot because of her injuries. The animals were buried in lye for a faster decay of the bones and hooves. March came in blustery and cold, but the sun was shining. The children got a few days outside, although the mud was deep in places, and she had to carry Prissy over the worst spots to find the remains of last year's grass. Nicolas didn't try the windmill again. Each time they went that direction, he gave it a wide berth. Finally, the warm southerly winds brought rain, the grass turned a pale green and the cattle, horses, and other animals thrived on it. Three foals were born over the course of two spring weeks.

Elizabeth continued to grieve for her lost little one. It was an emptiness she could hardly bear. When Nicolas ran through the yard yelling with joy, it ripped something from her, and Prissy, sweet Prissy, reminded her of what she might have had. Still, she settled her thoughts, hugged them at night and told them she loved them.

Elizabeth gave a birthday party in April for Nicky with cake and candles. Wilhelmina sent him toys and games. She and Lucas resumed relations, but it wasn't the same for him. As the anniversary of his wife's death came and went, he seemed moody and introspective.

"Lucas," she said to him one morning, while the children were playing outside in the warm sun. "What've I done wrong? Have I displeased you, somehow?" She no longer wanted to run away, for she knew she had nowhere to go. Not to the orphanage, certainly, for they had the small children to cope with. She couldn't get a position as teacher; she had no references.

Her only answer was a blank stare and red eyes. She tried to comfort him, while grieving herself over the lost babe. He spent many hours on horseback, riding his range to round up the cattle for branding the new calves, and for counting how many had been lost during the winter. She felt as if the four walls were caving in on her. Even the laughter of the children seemed to mock her; she had no child of her own to hold in her arms.

By June, the grass was tall and tender, the sun hot and dry, the cattle lazy in the pastures, and the new bull he bought from his neighbor who needed the money, frisky and ready to do his duty. Joey reveled in the summer weather, running in the fields and rolling on his back. Nicholas had befriended the animal, and they often chased each other through the grass. It was one evening while the sun was setting in a magnificent glow of red, yellow, gold and purple, that Elizabeth told herself that she would stop feeling sorry for herself. Life was passing her by, and she had two children who needed her; and a husband who worked without ceasing.

With an inner strength, and the fortitude of a rancher's wife, she drew up her skirts and began a whirlwind of activity to keep her busy and help her forget the past. She took the mattresses off the beds and let them lie in the hot sun to kill any lingering germs or odor. She took the rugs to the clothesline and beat the dust out of them. She scrubbed the floors and the walls, and standing high on a make-shift ladder, cleaned the ceiling. She made it a game for the children, for they wanted to help.

She took everything from the shelves and closets and cleaned them as best she could. She laid some old newspapers on the floor and let the children paint with water colors. She was satisfied when the whole house smelled of lye soap and carbolic acid and sunshine. If the men disapproved, they didn't say anything, for the bad smells were soon replaced by baking bread, cinnamon and spiced apples, and pickles.

Everything from the garden was cooked, canned or hung in the root cellar for future use. Elizabeth spent hours walking with the children in single file, while she explained about the sky, the birds and the animals of the ranch. She pressed Lucas to spend more time with the children, and surprisingly, he did. He held Nicky tight in his arms, and he rode him around the yard on his horse; he drank tea from tiny cups while remarking on Prissy's pretty new dresses, sewn by his wife's hands. Slowly, with loving attention and good food and exercise, Lucas began to come out of his melancholy moods and laughed again.

July and August passed by in a hot, dry haze, and

Lucas and the neighboring ranchers and farmers began to worry about a drought. Elizabeth laughed; they seemed to bemoan the winter snows, the spring rains, and the dry season alike. Hank told her that was the way with the ranching business, never satisfied. She cooked a thick, juicy pot roast for dinner, and he said he was gaining weight on her good cooking.

Jed Masters the drummer came by in September to tell them that his mail order wife was expecting, and he'd decided to move back to New Orleans. His business was slacking off, and he needed to find a new line of work. He surprised Elizabeth and Lucas by giving Elizabeth a big hug, and told her it was the best thing that had happened in Montana for him, when she moved there from Chicago.

Elizabeth Thompson had been in Montana over a year when she discovered she was with child again. This time both she and Lucas were cautious and worried, but everything was fine, and she delivered a healthy boy on the tenth of May named Alexander and called Lexie. Nicholas was nearly five, and Elizabeth was teaching him his letters and numbers. Prissy was three and getting into as much mischief as she could manage on her fat little legs. Another winter and summer passed them by, then two more. By the time Nicholas was twelve years old, the ranch house was filled to the rafters with children. After Lexie, there was Amanda, and the twins Mark and Jennifer, then sweet, curly, blonde-haired Sarah came to bless the family.

— 8 —

The turn of the century was an exciting time. Electricity had made it to the ranch, a single line attached to a series of poles that stretched into the distance. For now, there was a single bulb hanging from the ceiling in the kitchen, one in the front room and one in the upstairs hallway. Lucas had split the line to put a light in the barn, although no one ever turned it on. He teased and said someday someone would invent an electric milking machine, and the expense of the wire to the barn would serve him well, then. A phone was in the main house, and it connected to the barn. It was a convenience, Elizabeth said, and well worth the expense, although she caught Hank once listening to a conversation with the neighbors. She marched to the barn and scolded him, and sheepishly he crept away, apologizing and red-faced with shame.

The whole family rode in the farm wagon to Helena to celebrate the turning of the new century. There were parades and speeches by the politicians, and a picnic in the park. At night, there were fireworks, and the bands played loud and long. It was the first time Elizabeth had seen the city close up for she had only been in the railroad station the first time she was there. They stayed three days and nights in the hotel, packed with farmers, merchants, politicians, old time settlers and newcomers. It reminded her of Chicago in her childhood.

Lucas rode in from the pastures one day in May to see a fancy new black motor car parked in his yard. A black mongrel they'd taken in when Joey passed ran up, nipping at the horse's ankles. "Back, Lucifer," he called sharply. The dog yelped and ran toward the barn. Lucas rode to the corral, wondering who might be calling on them. He knew only one person in the county who had an automobile, and this wasn't it. He dismounted, rubbed his horse down and looked up to see Wilhelmina Pierce walking toward him. Leaving the horse, he ran to her and grabbed her around her ample waist. She pulled back, tears in her eyes.

"Now, Luke, you stop that nonsense. I'm much too old to be grabbed by a man in bright daylight." He laughed and turned to see a whole passel of children come out the back door.

"Daddy, Mama said for us to get out from under her feet, so she can cook supper. Will you take us fishing? It's still light, and you said you'd take us the first good day, and the sun's shining, and Jinney's being whiny again." This was Lexie Thompson being his usual self at the age of eight years. Lucas gathered him in his arms, for he'd grown too tall to be lifted into the air and jostled.

"Son, I'm afraid we can't go fishing today. This is my sister, come to visit us. I'm anxious to hear all the gossip from Chicago." He turned the boy around, swatted him on the bottom and headed toward the house. "Now, run along and play."

"What's gsip, Daddy?" This was Mark, one of the twins, at age four. "Tell us."

"Son, gossip is talking, and you know you don't like to sit around and hear the men talking about the weather and the price of hay. Run along all of you, and don't go near the corral; that new horse is still wild." He watched as the children, four of them, turned toward the metal swing set under the tree limbs that he'd assembled for them last year.

Prissy walked up in her blue-checked calico dress, with a dirty apron covering it. She was ten and tended to be bossy with the younger ones. She'd grown tall and slender, now a few inches shorter than her mother. "I'll watch them, Daddy."

"Thank you, Daughter." He turned again toward the house, gathering Willie to his side.

"How are you, Willie? And, Sam; is he well? What brings you to Montana?" Lucas smiled and seemed very pleased.

"We came on a vacation, Luke. Can you image that husband of mine just up and said, 'Let's go to Montana this year, Willie.' We've been to Europe and New York, but never to see you. He plans to retire at the end of this year, and I think he wants to get away from the business for a time. He had that flare up last year with the heart. I worry about him, Luke. He needs to slow down."

By this time, they'd reached the steps into the house, and he held the door open for her. She marched in and went straight to the parlor where her husband Samuel was reading a business-oriented magazine he'd brought with him. He rose to greet them.

"Lucas, do tell me that all these children aren't yours." He smiled as he teased, and they shook hands.

"Yep, all seven. Nicky's away at school. There's no upper grade school here, and Elizabeth does her best with them, but at twelve years he needs a more formal education." He chuckled.

"May I ask what's funny?" Samuel rolled the magazine in his hand, tapping one end against his leg. "Do you like to have the boy gone for such a long period of time?"

"It's not that, Sam. I miss him when he's away. It's just that when one's gone, the others make enough noise to replace him. I'll have to find a good girl's boarding school for Prissy next year. She's quite grown-up. It's hard to grasp; it seems she was a baby just yesterday." He looked around the room.

"You looking for someone?"

"Where's Elizabeth?" Lucas could answer his own question, for he heard two-year-old Sarah running and screaming upstairs. "That's the baby, Sarah. She hates to have her hair combed or brushed, just like her older sister did at that age. It's a tangle of naturally blonde curls and usually has jam or syrup in it, for she's sometimes a messy eater."

"Elizabeth's upstairs with the little one. I do admire her courage, to live so isolated and take care of so many children." Wilhelmina's voice came from behind Lucas, where she'd been standing, listening to the men and looking around the room. "I was right to send that girl to you. I guess I best check on things in the women's part of the house." She walked toward the kitchen, not seeming at all put out because Elizabeth hadn't come to greet her at the door.

Lucas glanced at his sister, who was blinking a tear from her eye, her handkerchief in her hand. He asked Samuel, "Where'd that come from?"

"She's so sentimental." Samuel winked at his wife's soft heart.

"Sentimental? My sister, Willie? Not the girl I grew up with, Sam." Lucas nodded toward the kitchen where they could hear the sound of pots and pans clanging.

Both men laughed, of one accord on the matter.

— 9 —

Willie Pierce disappeared into the kitchen, away from the men. And women were supposed to be gossipy. Could she help it if she found her nieces and nephews to be charming? She was anxious to see her brother's wife, see if she was the same girl she remembered. Herself, she was certain she hadn't changed much in nine years, gained a little weight, maybe grayer hair, but still strong even when Sam accused her of being a social butterfly. She considered herself a perfect foil to quiet, studious Samuel Pierce. While he attended the business, she shopped and entertained her friends. Her only vice was the game of bridge. She'd taken it up several years back and played once a week, sometimes at her home, sometimes at one of the other players' houses. She loved to have the girls over for tea or dinner, where she could hear the latest gossip among the social elite of Chicago. Now, if she'd had children, she might have been a different person, altogether.

She looked for the tea kettle and found it, but had to search for the tea. One of the children, Mandy, she thought, came in the back door and slammed it, making Willie jump in fright.

"Where's Momma?" The girl stood with her hands on her hips, and Willie could see in the child the reflection of the orphan girl she'd picked out at the orphanage so many years ago. She remembered Elizabeth's vehement struggle against the marriage. From the way Lucas acted, she was certain the marriage had turned out well. And, this was Elizabeth's daughter. Well. Well.

"She's upstairs, child, with your sister. Now who might you be? I'm looking for the tea. Can you help me?"

"I'm Mandy. It's right there at your side," the girl smirked.

Willie turned quickly, and the tin fell on the floor, where about a spoonful of tea sprayed from the container. Flustered, she picked it up, laid it on the table and gazed at the girl with her special look for people who displeased her. Mandy backed out the door and ran for her sister. Willie went to the door to call her back, but the girl was gone.

"Silly girl. To be frightened at the least little thing, just like her mother." She sighed and continued making the tea. She found a damp cloth and mopped up the spilled tea.

She was sitting at the table sipping her tea when Elizabeth came down with a subdued Sarah. There were streaks of tears on Sarah's cheeks, but her sweet smile came out when she saw Willie. "Mama, come, come." She pulled her mother's hand. "Kitties, mama."

Elizabeth sighed, "There's a litter of kittens in the barn, and she wants to see them a dozen times a day. We may have to bring them in the house to have some peace. Did you find the tea alright, cream, sugar?"

Willie noted rather vainly that Elizabeth was much more confident and settled than when she'd stayed with the Pierce's right before her marriage. She had the look of a happily married woman, her face serene. She whispered to Sarah to go play with her dollies and be quiet.

Willie watched the little girl go into the corner of the

kitchen where there was a small child's cradle and a doll. It surely wasn't the same doll that Willie had sent with Elizabeth for Prissy so long ago, was it? It was well worn and had one eye poked out. Willie couldn't be certain it was the same doll, as she didn't recognize the dress it wore, for it was blue gingham, and the tiny apron over the dress was green. She would have known the doll if it wore the red and black satin with the white lace trim in which it was bought, for she'd picked it out because of the pretty dress.

"Elizabeth, is that the same doll . . .?" Willie gazed quizzically at her sister-in-law.

"For Prissy, all those years ago?" She laughed, with a mischievous sparkle in her eyes. "Of course. The girls never will let me throw it out. They love it so. It keeps me busy sewing new clothes for it."

"Didn't it have a red and black . . .?"

"Satin? It still does, but heaven help me if I remember where the dress might be. Willie, you do remember the strangest things. That dress was much too frivolous to let a year-old baby play with it. Although, looking back, Priscilla might have gotten some pleasure out of it. Instead, it's been packed away somewhere." Elizabeth shook her head at her own young foolishness.

She started cooking dinner, while the ladies chatted.

"You do enjoy this, don't you, dear? Having your own family and cooking for them every day." Willie reached for a piece of celery and nibbled it genteelly, the crunch satisfying to her ears.

"It's a pleasant habit, and I've gotten quite adapt at talking, cooking and watching the children at the same time." She looked at the older woman with a somber expression on her face. "My only regret is that there are no women to talk to, for at the orphanage there was always lots of company about. I do miss the Sunday afternoon tea parties. Here there are only men. And, my daughters, of course. That's why it's important that they go East to boarding school. How else will they learn the social graces?" She gave a great sigh. She took a cleaver and slammed it down into a thick shank of meat.

Occasionally, they could hear the rumble of male voices in the parlor and the cries of children outside, but they were comfortable in the kitchen. If Mrs. Hardesty, the matron at the orphanage, could have seen Elizabeth Thompson, she wouldn't have believed it possible, but Willie remembered that Mrs. Hardesty had gone to her reward many years ago.

Willie watched closely, estimating Elizabeth had gained at least twenty pounds since she was a teacher at the orphanage. She sighed. She guessed it was having so many children. In Chicago, she would have recommended that she go to the beauty salon and have her hair and nails done, and join an exercise club like the one in which she belonged, but on the ranch in the middle of Montana, it really didn't matter how she appeared, if Luke was happy, and he was. Willie had saved all his letters over the years, and they had hinted at his contentment with his wife and family. She relished the look on his face just now when he came from the corrals.

Willie sighed again. She'd wanted children, but it was not to be. She had a pleasant life, and Samuel was good to her; she had to let it go. She was blessed with good health, and enough money to enjoy the theaters, opera and busy life of the city. She would never have been able to endure a life in the wilds of Montana. And, if that recent episode with her niece, Mandy, was an indication, it was as well that she hadn't had children.

— 10 —

The meal turned into a noisy party. Elizabeth thought of feeding the children and sending them to play while the adults ate but turned down the notion. Lucas' family would see them in their natural state or not at all, she told herself. First one, then another of the children interrupted with some complaint or comment. Sarah dropped her dish on the floor. Lucas, with the calm acceptance of long time experience, picked it up and gave her a clean one. Lexie and Mark began to argue, and Elizabeth spoke one word, "Boys," and they were quiet for a few minutes.

Later that evening, Elizabeth watched her guests climb the stairs with a tiredness that belied their age. She found it amusing, for both Samuel and Willie Pierce were clearly exhausted when they went upstairs to the room assigned to them.

Retiring to her room, Elizabeth let her hair down and brushed it until it shone. She worried that the children had been too exuberant at dinner, but she wouldn't have had it otherwise. They lived on a ranch on the rolling plains of Montana. She'd tried to teach them manners and etiquette, but with so many children, it was hard to control them at all times.

She turned when the door was opened and her husband walked in, his clothes still smelling of horse. She supposed he had so enjoyed the talk with Sam Pierce that he'd forgotten to change.

"Husband, I see you feel the need of sleeping with the smell of your horses still on you."

"What?" Lucas gave her a puzzled look.

"Look at you. Or, rather smell you. It's obvious that you work on a ranch."

He reddened. "Ah, yes. The ranch, but you love me, don't you?" He pulled at his clothes.

"Come, Lucas, bring yourself and your horsy scent into my arms, for I wouldn't have you any other way." She beckoned him with her arms and a smile on her face.

Lucas strolled to where Elizabeth was sitting at the dressing table. He took the brush from her hand. He pulled her into his embrace and folded his large hands around her. "Elizabeth, darling, you are so beautiful." He kissed her ear, and Elizabeth rose to turn into his arms.

"I do love you so much, my darling," she whispered in his ear.

From outside the open window, a bright full moon shone in and around the room, as if to smile on the joy of the couple. Long after they had gone to sleep, it moved slowly over the dark sky, and the twinkling stars followed until it slipped over the horizon, and the pale pink of dawn painted the eastern sky.

— Epilogue —

Willie and Samuel Pierce stayed for two weeks on the ranch. Sam even learned to ride a horse. Willie and Lucas spent long hours talking of their childhood. The couple enjoyed the sounds of children laughing and left with only pleasant memories of their time at the ranch.

It was only after they left that Lucas felt he could share his life's story with his wife. Elizabeth learned the reason why he'd chosen a life of hard work in the western state. At the age of thirteen, his father tried to bend him to his will and disciplined him with a whip. Lucas stayed until his mother died, then left the luxury of the family home, never to return. He didn't go back for his father's funeral four years later. He was finished with discipline and society, its rules and restrictions. He first worked as a clerk in a lawyer's office in Springfield, Illinois, and on an oil well rig in Pennsylvania, and moved to North Dakota where he worked as manager of a ranch.

Lucas told her how Willie endured their father's dominance until she was rescued at age twenty-four by the gentle, quiet Samuel Pierce. She inherited the house in which they still lived when their father died. Although, their father wrote nothing in his will concerning his only son, generous Samuel Pierce agreed to pay an equal share to Lucas, and with the funds from his brother-in-law's generosity, he bought the ranch near the great mountains of the West.

Samuel Pierce died of a massive heart attack six months after they visited Montana. Willie continued to entertain her guests in the huge house until in her eighties. The house, its furnishings and art works were donated to charity after a trust fund was set up for each of the Thompson children. The girls, Priscilla, Amanda, Jennifer and Sarah were given an equal share of their aunt's jewelry and furs.

Lucas and Elizabeth had another child exactly nine months after the visit of his sister, Wilhelmina Pierce. They named him Samuel Fortune Thompson after his uncle.

The Education of Jackson Humboldt

— 1 —

"Jacky!" In the cool, Chicago, early spring evening, the youth's name was nearly swallowed by the whistle of the nearby L overhead train line. Down the alley, a cat screeched, and a metal can lid clanked as a man's voice yelled. Through an open window, a child's penny whistle piped a discordant melody, and a whiff of horse dung clung to the breeze.

"Oh, Cincinnatus," the youth muttered under his breath. It was his mother's voice, calling from the back door. Their row house opened to a narrow back yard, filled with his mother's flowers in summer, but winter burnt and overgrown just now. He'd come to the wood pile by the tool shed for a few fags for the kitchen stove and worked his cigar stash out of the hollow log at the bottom of the stack. Smoke wafted around his face, creating a cloud of grown-up maturity, so Jacky Humboldt believed. It was his way of proving he didn't have to be the goody-boy from his grade-school years any longer. He was sixteen and a man. He could smoke if he wanted. He took one last long drag on his cigar, dropped it to the ground next to the pile and stomped on it with his shoe heel. He stooped low and covered it with soil. He smelled the sleeve of his heavyweight wool plaid jacket and caught the sweet tobacco smell from the cigar. There was nothing for that. He'd found mints at Marsh's Grocery on the corner for a nickel. The tin said *Makes Your Breath Fresh Every Time.* He guessed it'd have to do. He took one from the small, oval-shaped tin in his pocket and put it in his mouth. He brushed at his clothing, hoping the smell of tobacco that lingered would be lessened if he beat it out.

"Jacky?" His mother's voice was louder, and it had a strident edge to it.

She's angry, he thought. It was nearing mealtime, and her wood box had run low. He hadn't brought in the kindling from the pile, which was his reason for being near the tool shed in the first place. He grabbed a pile of small, hand-hewed logs in his arms and walked toward the back door of the large, two-story house that was his home. At least carrying the wood might dilute the smell of the cigar. He went up the three steps, disappointed to discover the smell was stronger as he worked, as though he was still encased in the smoke. It was too late to undo his escapade beside the tool shed now. His best hope was being careful not to drop the wood as he opened the door. He worked one finger into the screen door handle and wedged himself between the screen and the door. Through the two leaded-glass inserts, he could see into the back hall to his mother in the kitchen checking the firebox in the massive iron stove on which she prepared their meals. He crouched to grasp the knob in one hand and twisted, pressing on the door gently with his knee until it just began to swing free. Pushing it aside using his shoulder, he turned and gave it a shove with his foot before walking in to the pleasant smell of bread baking and a roast in the oven.

"Oh, Cincinnatus," he muttered a second time. His father, Nathan Humboldt, was home early from work, standing beside the stove talking with his mother, Mattie, and that was never a good thing. He wondered if his cigar forays had been discovered. Maybe Suzie Miller from across the alley had seen him. She tattled on everything. If his father demanded his stash, did he have enough money to buy more? Or perhaps Frank Travis could steal a few from his grandfather. He kept whole boxes of them in his bottom desk drawer. He watched his father hand his mother a piece of paper, and she folded it and placed it in the pocket of her apron.

"Hello, Papa." Jacky made his voice bright, as if he was happy to see his father. His parents looked at him, startled, and he realized they hadn't heard him come in. "How was work today? It's getting cold out there. I brought more wood in so Mother will have plenty."

He side-stepped the man and dropped the kindling into the wood box near the stove. He caught a glimpse of the cat, Boswell, beside the stove before he rose and moved from his warm spot to one farther from the noisy ruckus. Jacky stood, prepared to be called to task by his mother for being late bringing in the wood but was stopped by the look on his father's face.

"Sit down, Jackson."

His father's voice was low and gravelly, with no warmth. Jacky knew that tone of voice and sat meekly on the edge of the bench at the table, hoping beyond hope the cigar smell stayed within his jacket. He was in for it, now, he thought. He glanced at his mother, but she had moved to stand in front of the window, her hands hanging limply at her side.

"Son, there's something important that your mother and I have to say to you." His father cleared his throat. He looked at his wife, and she turned to look outside, fighting to control her expression. Jacky's father turned back to him, pressing his lips into a thin line.

For the first time, Jacky could see the gray tone of skin, the wrinkles in his father's face, and he was frightened. Nathan Humboldt was dressed in his dark blue conductor's suit with the tiny gold shield on the lapel that represented his authority with the Chicago Transit Company. The matching bronze buttons stood in contrast to the darkness of the cloth. His shirt collar was stiff and seemed to pinch his throat, and his tie had a small white spot near the place where it hung over his vest.

His mother withdrew from the window and sat in the chair across from him. Her rose-colored cotton dress was almost hidden under the bib and wide skirt of the stark white apron she wore when in the kitchen. Her hair was still a deep reddish-brown with few touches of gray and piled high on her head; a single stray strand had come loose, and she impatiently tucked it behind her ear. Her eyes were turned away, and she nervously bunched the end of the apron with one hand. Jacky quickly looked back at his father.

"I won't go into all the details now, but it's like this, Jackson. You have to go away."

At his father's words, his mother choked back a sob. As if needing something to occupy her hands, she stood, pushed the heavy chair noisily across the black-and-white checked linoleum floor and opened the stove's firebox to drop several small pieces of wood inside. The kitchen was quite warm, and she wiped her face with the hem of her apron before opening the oven to check on her roast.

Jacky took in her actions and gulped. He locked his eyes on his father and whispered, "Go away, sir? But, where am I to go?" He looked at his mother's profile and saw a tear roll down her cheek. He had trouble swallowing the lump in his throat. Frank and Suzie. Sure, Suzie was a tattler, but she was pretty, and he'd hoped she'd be his girl for the summer. There was riding the rail up to Lake

Michigan, maybe swimming for the day, and sneaking rides on the L. Everyone did that, if they were sixteen, anyway. How could he miss that? Would he be back by fall? Would he be coming back at all? He wished he'd never smoked those cigars. Maybe if he apologized, his father would change his mind.

He flinched when his father spoke, and he turned his attention back to him.

"Do you remember that your mother has an uncle by the name of Cloyd Fellows that lives on a ranch in Wyoming?" Nathan sat down at the table and took a deep breath.

"Yes, sir. He raises cattle and horses, doesn't he?" Wyoming? Oh, Cincinnatus, what was his father implying? He knew his uncle and aunt only from the picture mounted on the wall in his parents' bedroom. The tall, slender, dark-haired woman was standing with her hand on the shoulder of the man, stiff and somber, dressed in a dark suit and white shirt, his mustache almost covering his lower jaw. Jacky shuddered.

"That's right. He moved west after the war and built a large cattle spread near the border with Colorado. I've never been there, but your mother visited several times when you were just a boy."

"But, what does that have to do with me leaving Chicago?" His heart beating fast and his pulse racing to keep up, Jacky knew the answer from the quick peek he took of his mother's face. They had decided to send him to the ranch. But, he knew nothing about ranching, cattle or horses.

His father sighed, fidgeted with his tie and finally stuffed it inside his vest. Jacky's stomach began to roil, and he thought he'd be sick. To keep himself steady, he studied the grains of wood on the table top. It was almost gray from the scrubbing it had endured through the years.

He'd never noticed the square nail heads in the wood before now. He raised his head when his father began to talk, his voice low and deep.

"You won't know much about the investments that I made a couple of years ago, but the country's economy has gone into a slump. It's caught some of us unaware, and I've lost a great deal of money on the Exchange in New York. It'll put us back for a time. Your mother and I have discussed this, and there's no other way for it but to sell the house and most of the furniture and move into a rent house. Your mother wrote to her uncle and told him of the situation, and he's invited you to come and work for him for the summer."

"Work in Wyoming? But, Papa, I know nothing about cattle or horses." He spoke his troubling thought aloud. His mind kept returning to Frank and Suzie and the L and Lake Michigan under a cloudless sky. That concerned him even more.

"I know, son, but your uncle will teach you what you need to know. He takes on several temporary hands during the spring round-up, your mother says. Isn't that right, Mattie?"

"Yes, that's right." She sat beside Jacky and took his hand in hers, gently rubbing it as if trying to soften her husband's words. Her eyes were red, and her smile was shaky. "They have to gather the cattle from among the trees and the creek beds, count and brand them, so Uncle Cloyd will know if he needs to thin the herd or sell them off. They need extra hands during the spring and summer, and he usually hires two or three men; you'll add to his crew. It's really a very pretty place, Jacky; you can see the mountains in the distance."

Jacky wasn't a kid. He saw what she was doing, trying to convince him he'd love it. He wouldn't. He just wouldn't. It would be awful to be away from the city. He recognized the dreamy smile on his mother's face, picturing the ranch in her mind the way she remembered it. Beauty wasn't the reason he would be there. It got hot in summer, and riding horses? Would he have to saddle one? He'd never done that. And cattle were big. He'd been to the meatpacking district once. They were loud and noisy, and he wanted nothing to do with them. It would be hard work, and he wasn't accustomed to working with his hands. He looked at his neatly shaped fingernails and his soft hands. He examined the lines on his palms and was brought from his wandering thoughts by his father's voice.

"Well, your mother and I can't see any other solution at the moment to our problem. Maybe, by the end of summer, I'll have gained enough funds so that you can come back and finish school. A little hard work never hurt a man, and you'll get to know your relations better. Best look on the bright side, eh, son?" Nathan slapped the tabletop sharply. A glass butter dish jumped, and Mattie reseated the lid.

"Yes, sir. When do I need to go?" Jacky felt he'd throw up. Did he at least have time to say goodbye to his friends?

"Oh, it'll be a couple of weeks, surely. You'll need to talk to the teacher at your school and pay any expenses you owe for the library books you borrowed and things like that. I'll see about the train tickets, and your mother will take care of cleaning your best suit and underwear. Think of it as an adventure and new experience, and you'll be fine, I'm sure. Now, off with you to wash up. Your mother says the meal is about ready, and you'll be setting the table tonight."

His father turned toward his mother, and they began to discuss plans for the future, but Andrew Jackson Humboldt had ceased to listen. He didn't go wash up. He went out, sat on the back steps and felt the sting of tears in his eyes. He'd never been away from home before; not without his parents to guide him. What would it be like to live with strangers in Wyoming? He stood in the gathering darkness and made his way to the tool shed. With the toe of his shoe, he dug in the soil and picked up the dirt-covered cigar he hadn't finished. He flicked off the dirt and thought of smoking it, but held it in his hand, unlit. Somehow, the small act of rebellion and defiance against his parents no longer mattered. He threw it back down and packed the soil over it as before. He waited until his mother called him to supper, his head in a whirl of anticipation and fear.

— 2 —

Jackson Humboldt stood on the platform of Grand Central Station. The waiting room had been a marble wonder with massive columns holding up a coffered ceiling. He hadn't noticed. Now he clutched his ticket in one hand and a basket of food in the other, while his heart raced and seemed too large for his chest. Above the hiss of the steam engines and the clanking of metal against metal, people talked loudly. One couple was kissing just down from them, and the other direction, a young woman leaned out of the train window and laughed as a young man tried to catch the rose petals she threw his way. Jacky turned to kiss his mother's cheek one last time. He shook hands with his father and promised to write. He handed the ticket to the train attendant, went up the steps and down the hallway, and found a seat where he could see his parents through the smudged window pane. His mother was craning her head to find him inside the coach, but the windows were too cloudy. He took out a white kerchief and waved, but they turned away, not noticing his gesture of farewell.

The padded velour seats seemed to go on forever in

front of him. A wire rack overhead seemed too small for much of anything except a lady's handbag. The empty seats became filled as other passengers dragged their cases along the floor and dropped into their chosen locations along the aisle. He thrust his ticket stub in his pocket where he could find it if needed again and frowned. He slid his dark wool coat from his shoulders and threw it onto the seat next to him. He could hear the release of steam from the massive boilers and the faint sound of a train whistle above the chattering of the people's voices. He put the rush basket at his feet and hoped no one would sit beside him. He'd been told by his father, who had ridden a train before, that if he could claim the entire seat, he'd have room to stretch out and sleep in the coach.

He admired the wide space between the seats. The covering was a dark hunter green, almost black, and he ran his thumb over the velvety surface, bringing the lighter green shade to the smooth surface, and was pleased at the softness. The window curtains were a lighter shade of green, and were tied back with a gold braided cord. He poked his nose to the glass and looked down at the gravel and dirt near the iron rail. He could see bits of paper, straw, and a few larger stones along the grassy verge near the terminal. He laughed at the antics of a man who was frantically trying to hold his hat on his head against the wind, and with the other hand clutching a large bag and walking stick. The man walked briskly out of his sight, and Jacky turned around to steady the basket at his feet as the train jerked forward.

His mother had placed a thin cotton throw rug over the food that he could use to cover himself in the night if he was cold, she told him. He watched the other passengers file down the aisle and hoped he wouldn't be sick as the sound of the whistle came louder to his ears. The people began to quiet down, and he looked out the window at a few stragglers. His parents had left the platform and he was truly on his own.

Jacky could feel the tug of the coach as the engine began to pull away from the station. He watched the shadows creep along the sides of the buildings as the train began to pick up speed faster and faster, until the buildings were gone and only the open grassy fields and farm houses passing by were visible. He felt the presence of someone and looked up.

There stood a giant, burly man, his face covered in dark facial hair, his clothes wrinkled and his hat clamped flat against his ears. His coat was an olive herringbone tweed, with darker, striped pants of similar material. Jacky couldn't see his jacket underneath his coat but supposed it matched his pants. His pockets bulged with unknown materials, and a watch fob dangled across his paunch. His eyes were pale and piercing as he gazed down at the boy.

"That's my seat." He exclaimed in a deep, nasal tone. He took several audible breaths and grabbed the back of the seat to steady himself.

"Oh, I'm sorry. No one was here when I came on board the train."

"Don't matter." The man shifted his bulk, coming closer, as if to intimidate Jacky. His movement sent forth an aroma of garlic and onions. He leaned down to speak, and the smell of beer carried with his words. "Just move the basket and I'll sit beside you here. I don't mind losing the window seat, but I need room for my feet, you see." Jacky scrambled to move the basket from the man's path, but he growled, "Here, give it to me and I'll put it on top."

Jacky pulled the basket out and the man disposed of it in the narrow overhead rack. It barely fit, and the man had to give the base of the basket a good whack to make it go in. The youth hadn't thought of using the rack for that purpose. He pulled his wool coat close to him, bunched it up for a buffer in the seat and took a quick glance out the window in embarrassment, as the man removed his coat and hat and thrust them on the rack beside the basket. He sat down, adjusted his tie and pulled at his trouser leg, trying for more comfort. He paused a moment, then trust out his big, calloused hand. Jacky took it and gave it a quick shake, his thin, pale hand swallowed in the depth of the larger one.

"Name's Smith. Ned Smith. I know that's a common name, but it's the one I was stuck with when I came into the world. I'm not going far, only to Cedar Rapids. What you got in the basket?" The onion odor was less now that his coat was off, but the beer smell was stronger close up.

"Food. My mother said I'd get hungry on the trip and they didn't have the cash for me to buy something on the way." He looked down, his ears feeling warm as he admitted their reduced circumstances.

"Food, huh? That sounds good. We just had a food break, but it'll be morning before they make a long stop again. What kind of food have you got?" Ned smiled and motioned to the basket, as if in anticipation. He winked at Jacky before popping his tongue against the inside of his mouth.

"Huh, sausage, apples, bread, cheese." Jacky felt nervous; did the man expect him to share his food?

"You got a name, boy?" Smith was running his finger along the seam of his brown-striped pant leg. He reached in his jacket pocket and took out a spectacle case, and taking the wire framed glasses from the case, perched them on his nose and returned the case to his pocket. He raised an eyebrow over the rim and squinted at the boy.

"Yes, I'm Jackson Humboldt. From Chicago. My father's a street car conductor." He couldn't help but show his pride in his father's occupation, even if he had recently taken a loss on the New York Exchange.

"Chicago? I'm just passing through on the way to Iowa. Never much cared for the city; but the Sears, Roebuck store is a grand place for men like me. I can get my merchandise cheap from them, but they're about to run me out of business with the new catalog. I sell hardware and pots and pans to the farmers' wives. Don't usually take the train, but I've got a business meeting in Cedar Rapids on Monday. Train seemed the fastest way to get there. It's slow, but it's steady when a fellow goes on a long trip. You ever seen the Sears catalog? I got one in my bag, 'iffen you haven't seen it before." He reached into an inside coat pocket and withdrew a small order book and pencil. He seemed to relax in his seat, tapped the pencil against the book and prepared to go into details. Jacky didn't know how to stop him, so he listened politely until the man finally became quiet and seemed to doze in his seat.

— 3 —

Jacky jerked awake, his senses instantly taking in the sounds and smells of the train. He was alone in his seat, and he remembered that the large man named Smith had left the train hours ago. He pushed at his coat to spread it out and discovered underneath that Smith had left his Sears catalog behind. There was nothing to do for it, and Jacky enjoyed looking at the advertisements. Earlier, he'd pulled his basket from the top rack and eaten a light supper of sausage, cheese and bread before putting the basket beside his feet again, hoping it would discourage any other passenger from sitting next to him. So far, it had worked as the train moved slowly through the night. He took the throw from his shoulders and walked up the aisle to the facilities at the end of the car; as primitive as they were, it relieved the pressure on his bowels. The coach car was almost empty as it glided through the open fields, and the only light came from a small sconce on the wall holding a candle. Pressing his face to the window, he saw the moon overhead. It seemed to move along the black horizon, although he realized it was the train moving, instead. He took his seat again but couldn't sleep; his thoughts raced back to his home and childhood.

He took the pen knife from his pocket and lifted the lid of the basket. He found the cheese, cut a sliver and re-wrapped it tightly in its canvas covering. He pinched off a bit of bread and held it between his lips while he replaced the lid and slid the basket back under his feet. The cheese smelled good, and the scent drifted around his head. He chewed the bread and wished he had a glass of cider or beer to top it off. He slowly drifted back to sleep.

"Boy, heh, boy. This is your stop." The conductor tugged at his shoulder, and Jacky awoke with a jerk. He looked around, and the sun was coming in the windows on the right side of the train.

"This is Cheyenne?" He felt odd. He still had the remnants of a dream in his head, and it seemed impossible that he could have already arrived at his destination.

"Yep. That's what your ticket says. Cheyenne. Time to get your things together. We'll be pulling into the station in about ten minutes." The attendant was already rushing down the aisle to awaken the other passengers who were getting off at Cheyenne.

Jacky rose and tugged his clothing into place, yanked the basket from between the seats and hefted it onto the aisle seat, where he wrapped the throw rug over the top of his almost-empty basket to protect the remaining food. He turned to see other passengers collecting their possessions and steadied himself as the train clanged along the tracks.

He heard the now-familiar whistle as the train ran along the track and began to slow. Jacky could see the outline of small shacks with dirt yards, chickens plucking in the grass and soil, and sheds with standing horses as they passed by the windows.

There was a mighty heave as the train came to a stop and the bustle of the people moved him down the aisle and toward the door, clutching his coat, the basket and his hat as he moved with the crowd, down the steps and out the door. He gave a silver coin to the attendant, who grinned at him, and looked around.

Only a couple of wagons and a carriage stood nearby. A few people in a cluster yelped out a greeting as an older couple moved down the steps behind him. He felt alone and didn't know what to do. He moved away from the tracks, and as he looked to the right, there was a man standing beside a wagon, holding a sign that said, "HUMBOLDT." He began to walk toward him, his basket bumping against his leg. He set it down and turned to the man.

"I'm Jackson Humboldt."

The man was middle-aged, grizzled and had a full beard; he looked average in height and had a slight paunch behind his belt buckle.

"You got any more luggage, young man?"

"Ah, yes, I do." He laid the basket on the ground beside the wagon and searched in his pocket for his ticket. The man turned and walked toward the baggage car. The other passengers were waiting for an attendant in a blue suit, his jaunty red cap revealing his identity. Jacky moved to stand beside the stranger, and when his number was announced, presented his ticket stub to the attendant, who checked the name on the label of the baggage. Jacky lifted the heavy case and watched as the stranger took the trunk, hefted it onto his shoulder and headed to the wagon. There was only one box left, and Jacky went back for it after leaving his case beside his food basket.

Lifting the luggage one item at a time onto the wagon as though the pieces were bales of hay or cattle feed, the stranger tied them down with a heavy cord. He looked around at the train, now beginning to puff and pull as it prepared to move on down the tracks to the next station.

He turned to Jacky. "Jump aboard, young man. We got a ways to go, and I don't plan to spend the night in the open longer than I have to. I'm Flapjack Cornell, the cook and supply wrangler at the ranch. Your uncle said you plan to spend the summer working with us. Don't have to tell you, the men won't like the idea, you being a dude and all. But, I don't question what the boss says; I just cook the food and make sure the men have enough coffee to keep 'em happy." As he was talking, the stranger untied the horses' reins from the hitch post and stepped into the wagon.

Jacky scrambled into the passenger seat, hoping he could endure the months ahead of him.

"What's a dude?" he asked, holding his hat as the driver released the horses to move down the road. The dust was heavy in the air, and he sneezed, twice.

"A dude? Why that's a young'un like you; inexperienced and ignorant of the ways of cattle and men. You'll soon see; the boys are rough and hardworking, and don't you think they'll give you any slack as you learn the business. Me, I was raised on a ranch, so's I knew from the cradle what was expected; broke my leg 'bout ten years ago, and the boss said I was a cook from then on. I don't mess with the men, just see that their bellies are full and their bedrolls are cleans onct a week."

He seemed to have said all he wanted to say, so Jacky sat in silence through the rest of the trip, thinking of what Cornell had said.

— 4 —

The sun was low on the horizon, almost covered with dark clouds and streaks of red, orange and gold. The shadows stretched across the plains with long fingers of darkness beside the few trees standing as sentinels on the skyline. The heat of the day had cooled, and Jacky raised his coat collar around his ears, pulled the sides together and buttoned it. He stretched for the throw in the basket but couldn't reach it, so sat huddled against the chill air.

Cornell drove down a lane with trees on either side for a few yards and stopped in front of a rambling farm house, weathered with age and its front porch sagging under four columns. The roof was made of cedar shingles and had several patches of a lighter color. Jacky was most intrigued by the windmill, squealing and turning slowly with the change in wind direction. Underneath it was a large, round tin container of water, fed from the pump. Standing around were a few brown and white cattle and a horse.

A dog of medium size began to bark and twist and turn when it saw the wagon. Another large dog strained at the leash checking its momentum from attacking the wagon, as Cornell stopped the horses and stepped down. The first dog came to the wagon and began to sniff the wheels and contents of the wagon bed.

"Help me take in the luggage and put it in the spare room, until Tommy tells you what room to sleep in. I don't see no one around, meaning she's probably off for the day up to the Planter's house, given she and Sally Planter are close as flies on a cow's back." He chuckled at that, as if it were an open secret, and spat on the dirt. "The Boss is probably still with the cattle. I gotta start supper, or the boys'll be complaining." He tied the reins to a porch column, took the basket from the wagon and walked toward a shack standing alone beside a huge rectangular building.

Jacky took his time lifting his suitcase from the wagon and went up the steps of the house. Opening a heavy screen door, he stepped past, only to have it slam loudly behind him. He cursed, certain he'd make someone mad if he kept up such things. He'd have to be more careful. Leaving his suitcase just inside the door on the floor beside what looked to be a piano, he wondered what the man was going to do with his food basket. He shrugged his shoulders and looked about the room. To the left was a tall doorway that led down a hall. To the right was a massive fireplace. The room itself wasn't large and was filled with small tables covered with lace scarfs and ornaments. He picked up a replica of a shepherd boy and girl and laid it back down. The fireplace was made of large and small river rocks, from their smooth, rounded shape. It looked big enough to roast a whole cow; the ashes and coals were cold, and hanging from the mantle were various-sized utensils and a tea kettle. He'd love to have a cup of tea but dared not touch a thing. He could see the kitchen area from this angle but ignored it. He moved out of the room and down the hallway to open a door on the left; it was locked. He went to the next door; obviously a woman slept there, so he closed the door. He tried the adjacent door. The room was manly and had a massive bed and a large steer head mounted on the wall above a wood-burning stove; a desk or table was cluttered with papers, and a bookshelf contained several hefty tomes. There was a large, stuffed, leather-covered chair in the corner beside a small round table covered with a lace scarf and lamp. He crossed to the door across the hall and found a small room almost bare of furniture, with only an iron bedstead and table with wash basin and pitcher. A chair stood in front of the window. The bed was covered with a pretty quilt pieced in the colors of the rainbow, and he admired it for a second. The room boasted two windows and an outside door. He stepped to it and opened it onto a large, screened back porch that wrapped around the side of the house. He could see the barn and the cook shack to the right.

He retraced his steps, came back to the front room and was about to look more closely at the kitchen when he heard a great shout of anger, and several men rode their horses into the barnyard. The dogs from earlier began yipping in an excited manner. He stepped outside in time to see a large man with a red face and blue flannel shirt dismount his horse.

"Flapjack, get out here on the double." Jacky watched as the other men dismounted their horses and began to move toward the corral. Cornell came from the cook shack and, almost at a run, moved toward his boss. "What the hell do you mean, leaving the wagon and horses standing in the yard? How long you been here? Why aren't the supplies unloaded?" The man's face was blotched and his breath was coming in sharp, short pants. His companions ignored the goings-on as though the blustering was nothing unusual. Suddenly, he saw Jacky standing on the porch and let out a yell that would have echoed off the distant mountains if closer.

"Who are you?" He squinted into the sun. The

medium-size dog had trotted up to him, and he gave it a rough rub behind the ears. He started toward the house. Dust stirred with each hard step, and the horse jerked its head to the side, startled.

"I'm Andrew Jackson Humboldt, sir." Jacky stepped from the porch, his eyes watching for a reaction. He couldn't be certain this was his uncle, as he'd never met the man, but he did seem to be in a position of authority. He added, "Your great-nephew from Chicago."

"Hell. I forgot about you. Well, don't stand there; empty the wagon. Take the horses to the corral and give them a rub down." The man spun on his foot to walk away, glancing back to notice Jacky hadn't moved. He called to him, "Well? You waiting on an invitation to a party?"

Jacky stood stiffly for a moment, unsure how to take the cutting remark, and quietly replied, "I don't know about such things, sir. Could someone show me how to unhitch a wagon?"

A loud roar came from his uncle. "What? A relation of mine don't know how to unhitch a wagon?" Then, he stopped himself and began to laugh. He doubled over with mirth, and tears fell from his eyes. He took out a large red handkerchief from his pocket and wiped his eyes and face. "Nils, you and Patches, show the dude how to unhitch a team of horses and unload the supplies. We'll get this boy thinking like a ranch hand before too much of his life gets away. When you're done, boy, if this is your trunk, bring it in the house." With one last glance at his nephew, he walked up the steps and out of sight into the house. The screen door banged behind him with a loud smack of wood on wood.

Jacky looked up as the door banged shut. He walked to the wagon, climbed over the wheel and started to lift a box. At least, he knew how to do that. Cornell shot him a dark look, calling, "You didn't tell me you knew nothing 'bout unhitching a horse. You're a dude through and through." He disappeared into the cook shack, still muttering under his breath, and the other two men squatted in the dirt beside the wall. One of the men worked a plug of tobacco into a paper jacket, forming a rude cigarette, while the other rummaged in a pocket to come up with a small box of matches. He offered the matches to the man with the cigarette, who placed the freshly-made cigarette between his lips, and drawing in air as the match met the paper, lighted his smoke. It glowed brightly, then the man blew out a cloud of smoke. The second man retrieved his matches and began rolling one of his own. Jacky noted that smoking wasn't forbidden on the ranch, and he filed the fact away and moved a box to the back of the wagon, jumped down, turned and picked up the box. The men beside the wall only watched as he took the box to the front of the shack and laid it in the dirt in front of them. The loose dog had found shade under the wagon, and seeing the activity, meandered towards the smoking ranch hands and flopped at their side, exposing his belly for a rub. Jacky shook his head at the lazy animal, went back to the wagon and lifted a barrel, heavy and cumbersome, and repeated his efforts. He was puffing with exertion, and the men sat and watched, casually rolling more cigarettes and lighting the fresh ones from the end of the ones already burning. He struggled with his conscience; his uncle had told them to work, too, but they were letting him do the heavy lifting. Well, he'd show them. He went to the wagon, removed his box of books, placed it on the porch, went for the rest of his possessions and lined them up beside the box.

 Jacky used his sleeve to wipe the building sweat from his face. The two men, Nils and Patches, still squatted beside the wall, talking to each other. One of the men dropped the remains of his cigarette into the dirt and smashed it with the toe of his boot. Jacky snorted his disdain for the men, lifted a box and went up the steps. The inside was dim and cool, after the late afternoon sunshine. It was a large room with a long table in the middle and benches on either side. He put the box on the floor beside the door and went back for the other one. He could hear the sounds of laughter near the corral, but he ignored it and placed the other box beside the first one. He lifted the barrel and half rolled, half carried it up the steps and set it down.

"Hey, boy, what are you doing? Bring those into the supply room; you can't leave them there where the men'll fall over them." Once more, Jacky half rolled, half carried the barrel to where Flapjack Cornell pointed with a thin, pale finger and left it in a dark room near the kitchen area. He went back for the boxes, stacked them in the room and stood in the doorway watching as Flapjack stirred something good-smelling in the pot.

"That smells good. When do we eat?"

Cornell spun so fast he almost tripped over his long gray apron strings. The spoon dripped something red on the floor at his feet. "Dang, look at what ya' made me do, fool. You don't eat here, boy. You eat in the big house with the boss. This room's for the hired hands what work with the cattle." He took a wadded cloth from the counter and wiped the red sauce from the floor in two quick strokes.

"But, I'll be working with the cattle, won't I?"

The cook laughed. "You? Out, boy. I've got work to do, and talking to you don't get it done." He turned back to the stove, and began to stir the contents of the pot.

"Hey, what'd I do wrong?" It was bad enough he'd been banished from Chicago, and worse he was stranded in this godforsaken wasteland where it seemed he could do nothing right, but he'd done nothing to offend this man.

"Put me in a bad light, that's what. You should'a told me you'd not know how to unhitch the horses. Even city folks should know that." The man didn't turn around or look at Jacky.

"I'm a dude, remember?" Jacky snorted the words with a sour laugh. A moment of homesickness washed over him. The man didn't respond, and Jacky went outside and stood a moment, his thoughts in turmoil.

There was a noise from the lane, and he looked up. A man rode up on a large black stallion, stirring up dirt in front of the ranch hands. The leashed dog began to bark, while the lazy one roused from beside the ranch hands and trotted toward the horseman. Jacky turned to meet him. He was magnificent, tall with broad shoulders, wearing a black sombrero on his head. He jumped from the back of the horse.

"Hey, what the devil's going on? Why's the wagon still in the yard?" His voice was gruff, and he glanced around the yard, calling to the idle ranch hands. The dog pressed against his leg, and he pushed it away with his boot. His eyes widened when he saw Jacky standing in his city clothes and dusty shoes.

Jacky darted a glance at the house, but his uncle wasn't visible, and he was alone with the strangers.

"You? Who are you?" The dark-haired man looked at his companions near the corral for an answer, but they were silent, with their heads ducked, caught not working and trying not to be noticed. After he turned away, they stood, brushed their dungarees, sending dusty clouds into the air, and headed towards the horses to unhitch them and lead them to the corral.

"I'm Mr. Fellows' nephew. I came to work during the summer." Jacky smiled, trying to make the best of it.

"Nephew? He didn't say anything to me about no nephew comin' for the summer." The man had the horse's reins in his hand, and as he spoke, he looped it loosely over the hitching post. He called to the barking dog, "Hush, you," and it dropped its head and slunk off. He patted the horse's neck and clucked to it several times before giving Jacky his full attention.

"He didn't tell me about you either. Who are you?" Jacky was tired of being the butt of everyone's irritation.

"I'm Taylor Edmondson, the foreman of this ranch. What's your name?"

"I'm Jackson Humboldt."

"Umboldt? What kind of name is Umboldt? Sounds foreign to me." Edmondson pursed his lips and narrowed his eyes. He tilted his head back and looked down his nose at Jacky.

"It's my name. I'm from Chicago. And it's Humboldt, with an H." He felt his blood rising, and he clenched his hand.

"Well, it's a dumb name." The man snorted a sour chuckle, as if anyone should know that.

Without warning, Jacky let go a right fist to the man's face. Blood spurted from his nose. Edmondson flinched and recoiled, calling, "Why, you little—" and he lifted his hand for a swing at Jacky. The boy responded with a tight fist to the stomach, and the man buckled at the knees. Jacky left no time for him to react, but covered him like a quilt, his fists moving with almost lightning speed; right, left, right, into the gut. One of the men, Nils, came to separate them.

"Whoa, boy. Ain't no use for that." He grabbed one of Jacky's arms, nearly getting socked himself, and pulling his head back just in time. "Now, now, I ain't part of this all, and you don't go socking me, young'un. Don't need to make this a free-for-all. Mr. Edmondson there, he's a good guy once you get to know him." The whole time he talked, Nils patted dust off Jacky's clothing, and encouraged him by clucking the cheek on one side of his mouth.

Still angry and resentful, Jacky backed away,

brandishing an arm the direction of the man on the ground, who was moaning in distress. Out of the corner of an eye, Jacky saw his uncle standing on the porch and dropped his arm. He blinked twice and took in the scene around him. He realized he was surrounded by cowboys, Nils on his right and Patches on his left, holding him steady. Two other hands stood, watching, while his uncle came down the steps, his face contorted in rage.

"Jackson, go in the house." Jacky drew a kerchief from his pocket and wiped his face, gave one last look at his opponent on the ground and strode up the steps. Cloyd Fellows yelled at his men. "Damnation, Patches, what's going on here? Jake, take care of Edmondson's horse. You men know better than to leave animals standing in the yard." He frowned at the man lying on the ground, and he turned back to Jacky and followed him in the door. The man called Jake caught the reins of the black stallion and led him toward the corral. Edmondson rose, picked up his sombrero and followed.

Jacky was confused. If he wasn't to work with the cattle, then why was he here? Why hadn't his uncle told the hands who he was? He had no time for more introspection, as Cloyd closed the door behind them, and let loose a string of curses.

"Damn, not an hour on the ranch, and you're already fighting my men. I see why Mattie wrote to me. Well, no matter. Get cleaned up and change your shirt, can't have Tommy seeing you like this. I have to finish my paperwork, before I forget what I came in the house to do." He walked down the hall to the room with the books and large bed. The door slammed shut behind him.

Jacky was glad he'd done some exploring earlier, or he wouldn't know where the sink was located. He took his suitcase to the back bedroom and opened it to remove a shirt. He pulled off his soiled shirt, wadded it into a ball and threw it on the floor. Heading into the kitchen, he washed at the sink, using a bar of rough lye soap from an earthen bowl and drying his face and arms with a thin towel hanging on a hook. He crumpled the towel beside the sink and stood for a while, his hands on the edge of the sink, looking into the chipped, porcelain bowl. He was confused and afraid to go into the front room. Hearing the sound of horses outside, probably one of the horsemen, he jerked away, snatched up his clean shirt and slipped it on, buttoning the front from the bottom to the top. He tucked the tail in his pants and saw the fight had soiled them, also.

Was his father wrong? Had he not been invited to work on the ranch this summer? He glanced out the window and saw two more hands ride into the yard and dismount. They talked to Nils and Patches and looked toward the house. He opened a couple of cupboard doors and found the coffee tin, opened it and looked for a spoon. He saw the coffee pot on the range and went to the hand pump at the sink for some water. He was glad that at least that was familiar. Setting the filled pot on the stove to cook, he sat at the table with his head in his hands. He was hungry and wished he had his sausage and cheese, but the cook had taken the basket from him.

He heard the sound of wheels and glanced out the door. A woman in a large, broad-brimmed hat and in the pants and shirt of a male was driving a single horse drawn carriage to the entrance of the house. Jacky watched fascinated as she dropped the reins and climbed from the vehicle. She was tall and very slender; her long limbs were encased in denim with the cuffs rolled up at the ankles as if the pants were too long for her height. She reached in the back for a basket and lifted it out. Jacky pushed open the screen door, letting it slam behind him, and moved onto the porch. When she didn't seem to notice him, he ran to her.

"Let me carry that for you, ma'am." He flinched as the woman turned and snorted with disdain.

"I ain't feeble and weak. I can carry my own basket. Who are you?" She held the basket as she spoke to him, making no move to walk to the house. Her fist on the basket's handle showed sharply outlined tendons under the skin.

"I'm Jackson Humboldt, ma'am." Did no one know him? He felt as though he had stepped into a strange world where he was unknown, uninvited and most certainly unwelcome.

"You're Jackson?" She gazed at him a moment as though he were a strange animal she'd never encountered before. "Come in the house, then. You don't look much like your mother's picture."

"No, ma'am." Jacky meekly followed the woman into the house, where two men were heard arguing in the bedroom with the stuffed steer head. He wasn't sure of her welcome, but at least she hadn't yelled at him.

"Cloyd!" She muttered as she tried to maneuver the basket and unstick some paperwork from inside one of the pockets of her denim pants. "Damn. Just like that husband of mine; foist his nephew on me, then don't tell me when he's coming." In the same tone but louder, she turned to Jacky, as if noticing he'd followed her inside. "Take this basket in the kitchen." She thrust it at him.

"Yes, ma'am." He took the basket and walked to the kitchen, setting it on the long, wooden kitchen table. He checked the coffee to see how it was coming. The scent of the coffee brewing must have permeated the house, for Jacky heard the sound of footsteps coming down the hallway. He braced himself, thinking it was his uncle, and half expecting to be taken back to the train station before nightfall. But, it was his aunt. She had removed her hat and taken off her gloves.

"Ummm. That smells good." She went to the cupboard and reached for a cup. Paying no attention to the boy standing at the table, she poured a cup of coffee and took a sip. "You can have that room at the end of the hall, the one that opens onto the back porch. I expect you to pick up after yourself and keep the room clean. I ain't got time for my work and yours, too. The outhouse and the bath is that small building near the cook shack; everyone uses it but me. I have my own facilities in my room. Now, get out of my kitchen so I can start dinner."

Feeling dismissed, Jacky walked to the front room, but it was empty. He was alone in a strange house in a strange land with strange people. He picked up his trunk and took it to the small room indicated. He set it beside his suitcase and went back for his box of books and pictures. He opened a door and saw that it was a closet. He began to unpack. Each item promised to bring tears to his eyes, but he refused to give in to his misery.

— 5 —

About an hour later, he was deeply engrossed in the antics of a private detective in one of his dime novels when he heard a bellow from the kitchen. The protagonist had been stalking a thief through the slums of London, a man who stole small children from the streets and sold them into slavery as chimney sweeps or domestic servants, and for a moment, he had trouble reorienting himself to his surroundings.

"*Jackson.*" The call came again, louder.

He put the book down and walked down the hallway to the kitchen. His aunt was standing over the stove, her apron spotted with stains, and his uncle sat, a frown on his face, as though he was still angry over the afternoon's activities.

"Yes, sir?" When they looked at him without answering, he looked at his clothing and found his shirt was still clean and neatly tucked. He looked up and realized there were plates on the table.

"Well, you want food? Wash up," his aunt instructed.

Jacky went to the sink, manned the pump and ran some water, washed his hands and sat on a bench at the table.

The table was set for three people, the utensils gleaming in the light from a lantern in the center of the table. A red-checkered cloth covered the whole. There was a covered soup tureen near the man sitting at the head, the spoon peeking from a hole in the lid. There was a platter of fresh bread nearby, and the aroma made Jacky's mouth water. On the other side of the lantern, a plate of bright yellow corn-on-the-cob sat dripping with butter. Jacky had time to note the plate had a small chip at the rim, before his aunt turned with a pot, and holding it between her hands with a cloth, she dropped it onto the table in front of him.

"There. Dig in before it gets cold. I'll get the pie from the oven." She turned back to the giant stove and followed her words with action. His uncle didn't wait. He lifted the lid from the tureen and began to dip a large spoonful of the contents into a bowl.

Jacky watched quietly, then blurted before he could think what he was saying.

"Don't you say grace?" He looked at his uncle with confusion.

"Grace? Don't need to thank the Lord for what I done myself. Look at the garden; I planted the corn and the beans and 'taters. Took the grain down to Sillars' mill for the grinding in my own wagon, too."

"Oh," Jacky responded in a timid voice. He rose to spoon some soup into the bowl on top of his own plate. He saw his aunt place the pie, steaming from the oven, on the counter, and turn toward him with a surprised look on her face, but she said nothing. She came around the table and sat at the opposite end from her husband.

She handed Jacky her bowl; he dipped some soup into it, and they began to eat. Silence reigned as the meal was consumed. The soup was finished, the bowls set aside, the meat carved and the corn and boiled potatoes consumed, before his uncle began to talk.

"I wrote to Mattie to say you could come until your father gets his finances in shape again. He always was a big investor in the 'Change. Was bound to lose a large sum sooner or later. But, I don't hold that against him; lost some money myself a few years back. Had a terrible drought that summer and the hay crop was lost. Had to buy from my neighbors. I need help 'bout this time of year; always hire two or three extra hands." He wiped his mouth with his napkin and sighed, taking time to push a few things around on the table before looking up at Jacky.

"The thing is, Jackson, your mother said you was good at mathematics. And, have a good knowledge of reading and history. That's mostly what we need you for, not working out on the ranch. I knew you, being city bred, would likely not know much about that. My wife there, she never learned to read and write and cipher. I figured with you living in the house, you could do my paperwork and teach the old gal how to do those things."

Jacky glanced at his aunt. She had her head low in her shirt collar, embarrassed by her husband's words. His uncle continued to speak, and Jacky looked at him.

"Now, it won't do for you to stay in the house all the time, else the boys'll begin to wonder why you're not with the cows. They don't cotton much to sissies or those who laze around letting others do jobs for 'em. They know you're city, so they been planning on ways to teach you how to be a real ranch hand. Can't let them down. Besides, some of them cain't read or write either, and I suspect they might take offense to you tutoring Tommy, when there's other work to be done. So, here's what we'll do. During the days, you'll learn to ride and work with them at the corral. I expect Edmondson will be quick to set you straight when you don't know something, but Jackson, you done dug a hole there." He paused and cleared his throat.

"Yes sir." Jacky had forgotten the man's name in the

violence of the outburst, but his uncle saying it brought it all back. It still made him angry. He'd stand up to him again if he had to, and he clenched his fist under the table.

"I see you're still angry, but that's not his fault." Jacky's uncle paused, then started again. "Didn't start off like I hoped, you getting into a fight with the foreman the first thing. He didn't take that well, but I told him you'll take orders like the other men, and he won't have no more trouble. I want your promise on that, or you'll pack and go back to Chicago tomorrow. I can't have my men thinking you're spoiled and a bully."

Jacky looked at his uncle, his thoughts darting around like pebbles in a bottle when shaken. He glanced at his aunt, who had begun to eat again. She wouldn't look at him. Something wasn't right, he could feel it. He suspected the couple didn't like each other much. There were those two bedrooms, one feminine; the other masculine. The woman dressed like a man, even now at the supper table. And she had her private bathroom no one else was allowed to use. His mother was always well-dressed and tidy; his father liked her to wear women's things.

"Very well, Uncle. I'll try to act like a gentleman, but I don't know anything about horses or cattle or unhitching wagons. I was tops in my class at school, so I can teach you, Aunt, to read and write, if you're willing to learn. I suppose this is a secret from the men?"

"Yes. Not even my best friend, Sally Planter, knows, but she suspects it, I think. I can't answer her questions when she talks about books and shopping." She gave her husband an appealing glance, and Jacky wondered if that was the reason they lived separately, while in the same house.

"Don't worry, Aunt, you'll soon learn." Jacky hadn't brought things to teach with, except his paper and his dime novels. Oh, and the catalog. He could teach arithmetic from that. His mind was already running, planning how he could do this; and he felt better already. "Probably sooner than I learn about staying on a horse." He laughed and was pleased to see that his uncle laughed with him. His aunt ducked her head, but then a sweet smile crossed her face, and Jacky thought she had beautiful soft gray eyes. He took a chance and placed his hand over hers and patted it in sympathy.

She rose from the table, cut the pie into large slices and gave the men a sliver of the dessert. It was very good, and Jacky was beginning to see that even if she couldn't read or write, she was a good housekeeper and cook.

"Come with me to the bunkhouse. The boys are probably finished eating. It don't matter, I need to speak to the men about you. Explain who you are; but not why you're really here. Now, I told your mother, I'd pay you twenty dollars a month, five for yourself, and the rest to send to your parents for their care while you're here. You'll have plenty to eat and clean clothes and a place to sleep, but the rest is up to you. You get out of line again, like this afternoon, and you'll be on the train before the next morning. Is that clear, boy?"

"Yes, sir. That's clear." The men rose and went to the room with the books and large bed. It was obviously used as an office. With the books on the shelf, Jacky wondered why his uncle hadn't taught his wife how to read before this. They walked out the door and into the star-studded night.

A light was shining from the open door and windows of the bunkhouse and the separate cook shack; the smell of cooking smoke, fried meat and coffee blended with the scent of horses, and dust filled Jacky's nostrils as they crossed the yard and entered the door. The table in the center of the room was bare, with the remnants of the men's meal spread across it; the men looked up and were instantly quiet when the boss entered the room, followed by his nephew.

"Hello, boys. Go ahead and eat; I didn't come to interrupt you." Jacky glanced at the head of the table and saw the puffed eyes, the hint of a cut lip on the face of the foreman, before he took a stance behind and to the side of his uncle. He could sense the hostility in the men, and his shoulders rose in defiance.

The men, in spite of his words, dropped their spoons or forks and stared at Jacky; the two men he hadn't met, one a rangy, balding redhead with the bottom half of his face brightly burned and the other swarthy with a graying beard, glared at him with resentment or anger, Jacky couldn't tell. Cornell, the cook, kept eating. He refused to look at Jacky. Edmondson, the foreman, glanced at his men, as if for support, then sat quietly as Cloyd Fellows began to explain.

"This here is my great-nephew, Jackson Humboldt. He's from Chicago, and his pa decided he needed to learn about the Wild West." He grimaced and continued. "Not that it's so wild anymore; but it's something outside his kin; he's a city boy. I expect you to treat him like any other dude from the East; teach him what he doesn't know, but don't think he'll shrink from the work, for he's a man and my relation. Now, he has a word to say to you."

Jacky was surprised, his uncle had said nothing about a speech, but he looked each man in the eyes for a second and finally came to the foreman at the head of the table.

"I apologize for my behavior this afternoon. And, especially to you, Mr. Edmonson, for making it personal." Jacky took a breath, having done what his uncle said, but he couldn't stop there. He wouldn't be run over by these men. "But, understand this, all of you; my name is a proud one. The Humboldts have been in this country for a hundred years or more, and my father is a respected and honorable man. He's a street car conductor in Chicago, and I won't listen to anyone who doesn't accept that fact." He stared at Edmondson until the man looked down at the table, and he continued, "I can understand your surprise and doubts about me. I expect it. I'm a stranger. But, I want to learn, and I hope you'll teach me about the West, like my uncle says." He grinned and looked at Cornell, the only one whom he expected to support him. His grin was received with silence and dark, gloomy looks. Hurt, Jacky puffed up, and he walked out of the room and left his uncle to finish the discussion as he saw fit.

Outside the door, he could hear the angry sound of raised voices from the men inside. He walked to the corral and stood with one foot on the lowest rail. He took a deep breath, wishing he had a cigar; but he hadn't brought any with him. He looked up at the sliver of a moon and the stars, more than he had possibly seen in his lifetime. He sighed. Facing a summer of loneliness and confrontation overwhelmed him for a moment. He dabbed at his eyes with his sleeve. He walked to the back door that led into his room, shut the door behind him, reached for the key and locked it, placing the key on his table. He felt his way in the dark, plopped on the bed and stared at the ceiling. His face felt stiff, and the few cuts he had received during the fight bothered him, but he ignored the pain. The sound of his uncle returning to the house came through the thin walls, and he heard raised voices coming from the front room. He covered his head with a pillow and let his loneliness and shame bleed from his eyes until he fell asleep.

— 6 —

Jacky awoke to the sound of a loud knock on his door. He opened his eyes to the sight of an unfamiliar room. A small crack of light showed at the bottom of the door coming from the hallway, and he realized he'd fallen asleep in his clothes. He cursed at the night air and rose and lighted the lantern. He gazed around and saw his trunk only half unpacked. The dime novel he'd been reading the afternoon before lay face down on the table beside his room key. He made a short trip to the outhouse and drew some water to wash his face and hands. He longed for a bath but could smell the scent of coffee and bacon frying and knew he didn't have time. Back in his room, he donned clean clothes, leaving his soiled ones on the floor beside the bloody shirt from yesterday. He chuckled to himself as he thought of what his mother would have said had she seen them. But, he quickly sobered, strode to the kitchen and paused at the door. Just as the night before, his aunt was at the stove and his uncle eating at the table, silence between them.

"Good morning, folks." He walked to his aunt and kissed her on the cheek as he would have greeted his mother, had he been home. She flinched, turning to watch him as he confronted his uncle. "Good morning, Uncle. What's on the agenda for the morning? Do I saddle a pony and ride to the far pasture or dig fence holes near the barn?" He laughed, hoping for a pleasant rejoinder. But, he was met by silence. Not letting it deter him, he lifted his napkin onto his lap, bowed his head, said a short prayer and reached for the bacon. "Umm, this smells good, ma'am. Do we raise our own pigs, Uncle? You said something about the crops; who tills the garden? How many men work for you?" He ate the bacon and reached for another piece. He saw a platter of biscuits and a small jar of what looked like honey. He dipped his spoon into it and sighed with anticipation.

"How many eggs do you want?" A small, timid voice asked. He looked at his aunt and grinned.

"I'll have three, if that's not too many. Shall I have to collect the eggs while I'm here? Will I have time to explore the area this morning?" Still not deterred from his efforts to raise a welcome from their faces, he began to eat his biscuit, covered in melting butter and dripping with honey.

Suddenly, his uncle laid his napkin on the table beside his plate. "The pigs and chickens are beside the barn, along with a milk cow and some goats to keep the grass low around the yard. Yes, it's probably better that you stay near the house today, until the men get used to seeing you. I'll go to the bunkhouse and give Edmondson his orders for the day; and I'll show you around. There's a gentle old horse that you might learn to ride, if you're willing. We'll spend the morning on that, but I need to drive to the neighbor's house for a while." He finished his cup of coffee and rose to leave the house by the side door.

Jacky took a sip of coffee and ate his eggs, perfectly cooked the way he liked them. His aunt sat down, took a biscuit and buttered it. He wondered if this was their usual routine: cooking, eating and not talking.

"I don't want to embarrass you, ma'am, but why did you never learn to read or write? I saw some books in my uncle's office. Has he never attempted to teach you to read?"

She dropped her biscuit onto her plate. A look of panic crossed her face for a second and was gone. She looked at her plate. "There's been no opportunity. We've only been married a year. I was raised on a ranch not far from here, about thirty miles on the other side of Cheyenne. My mother died when I was born, and my father was always working in the pasture with the cattle; I was taught to cook and sew and take care of myself by an old Indian woman who spoke broken English. I never went to school, or had any friends to teach me."

"I'm sorry, but why didn't your father send you to boarding school? You could have learned there." He took another bite of bacon and chewed thoughtfully.

She ducked her head. "I guess he never thought of it." She seemed defensive, so Jacky decided to change the subject.

"How did you meet my uncle?"

She glanced at him and then away. "At a horse auction. My father and I brought about a dozen mustangs we'd caught in the cane breaks near our place for the sale, and Mr. Fellows bought a couple of them. He and my father arranged the marriage. Pa said I needed someone to care for me, as he was getting too old and planned to sell the ranch." There was a far-off look in her eyes.

"Is your father still alive?" He'd seen her expression and tried to be kind.

"No, he died in the winter. I think he knew he didn't have long to live; I talked to the doctor, and he said Pa had the cancer; he'd been ill for a long time. But, he never told me. I never suspected. Minnie, the Indian woman, said he was glad to see me settled; that was his main worry."

"Where's Minnie now?"

"She moved in with her daughter on the reservation. She's very old, eighty-five, and happy to live with her grandchildren and revert to the old customs. I miss her."

"What about your ranch? Does my uncle run cattle there, too?" He wondered how that worked, to own two ranches.

She rose suddenly and began to gather the dishes from her husband's place. Jacky thought she wouldn't say more, so took another biscuit to soften the silence in the room.

She took the dishes to the counter and pumped the handle until the water came, splashing onto her apron. She stepped back, then as though to clear the air, she turned, her slender figure and posture stiff but a determined look on her face.

"My father left me the ranch and the animals, but Mr. Fellows sold them. He said he couldn't take care of two ranches and them so far apart. I told him that was my home, my heritage, the place my grandfathers settled in the last century, but he was adamant. He put the money in the bank for our children. But, no children have come." She glared at Jacky, defiance in her eyes. "I married him, and the preacher said the words, but he don't touch me. I don't allow it. It pleases me to make him wait until I'm ready." She tossed her head and gave him a fierce look of rebellion.

Jacky didn't try to understand; he asked about his aunt, Gloria. "My mother doesn't seem to know about you. What's your name? What happened to Gloria, my aunt before your marriage?"

She gave him such a look of surprise; he was startled, in his turn.

"She died. Didn't he write your mother about it?"

"No, I thought you were Gloria; he never said he'd

remarried. My mother showed me the letter he wrote saying I could come here for the summer." His face reflected his puzzlement, and she must have sensed it. She began to laugh. She flopped onto a chair and raised her apron to her eyes, and he could see the emotions burst from her in the form of chuckles and squeaks.

Embarrassed himself, he began to take his dishes to the counter. He looked on the shelf, saw some lye soap and supposed she used it for the dishes. He saw a kettle on the range, filled it with water and placed a piece of kindling in the firebox to build up the heat in the stove. He turned. She was quiet, her face smooth, with all signs of emotion gone.

"He told my father he always wanted children, but his wife Gloria couldn't conceive; so he agreed to marry me. I only found out after the wedding that he sold the ranch and the animals; he kept a few of them, the bull and a half-dozen horses and the milk cow. The rest were all sold while I was on the reservation, getting Minnie settled with her daughter. When I came back, he told me what he'd done, and I agreed to live with him if he wouldn't ask for his marital rights. He hasn't asked." She walked to the counter and started finishing what he had started; she put some dishes in the large enamel pan, took the kettle from the stove and poured the hot water over them.

"Oh, Cincinnatus." Jacky's head spun at that. He didn't know how to respond. He shifted topics to cover his embarrassment. "Was it your idea to learn to read and write?"

"Oh, goodness, no. It was only after we were married that he found out. He said if I could read, then it wouldn't be so bad, living on the ranch with him. But, I love it; it's the only life I know. I like to ride and tend the cattle, but he won't let me. He says it's not a lady's place to work with the cattle. I'm not a lady."

She had her back to him as she said it, and Jacky watched her work at cleaning the dishes. She moved fast, scrubbing hard. He remembered his upbringing. He'd learned to live on the streets of Chicago and knew nothing about ranching. He supposed if she grew up on a ranch, surrounded by men and one Indian woman, she'd know nothing about being a lady like his mother. He considered where he was now and what he was expected to learn and decided if he could become even partly a ranch hand, he supposed she could learn to become a woman like his mother, if she had someone to teach her.

"I'll leave you to your chores, ma'am." He started to leave the room but remembered she'd never told him her name. "Ah, what's your name? What shall I call you?"

She turned and grinned, a look of surprise on her face. "I'm Tommy. My father named me after himself, Thomas Theodore Marlow. That's my name: Thomas Theodora Marlow Fellows." She laughed, and he quickly exited the room.

Jacky stopped by his room long enough to fetch a thin jacket. In spite of the fine, sunny morning, a slight chill was in the air. He couldn't decide what his parents would think about his aunt by marriage. He guessed his mother had never met her; she was much younger, although maybe they'd seen each other on one of her visits years before. He shrugged. He had no idea how far Tommy's old ranch was, so maybe not. He wondered whether he should write to his mother, but decided it would wait until later. He tried to think if he'd been told of Gloria's death, but was certain his parents didn't know.

He saw his uncle coming from the bunkhouse and walked to meet him. The two dogs trotted at his side, little clouds of dust stirring with each footstep. He could now, with his new knowledge, see the worry lines on his face, and the frustration that must reside in his heart and soul. To be married, yet not married, must be a terrible thing, thought the boy. He watched as the hands came from the bunkhouse, one at a time. They gave him timid looks, hostile looks and angry looks depending on whether he was forgiven for his fighting with their boss and friend. He smiled and held his head high. They scrambled to the corral, selected horses, saddled them and rode out of the yard, leaving only him and his uncle standing, as the cloud of dust settled over the grassy verge.

"Come with me." His uncle growled under his breath.

Together they walked across the yard in silence. It took a few minutes for Jacky to become accustomed to not being spoken to, as if he was being ignored. He was often irritated at his parents, but they never ignored him, even when he wished they would. He was seeing, in only one day, that what he'd had was better than what he had come to. They toured the barn, the pig pen, the chicken coop and fenced area and the hay fields nearby, walking briskly and with a stiff distance between them. At last, Cloyd stopped near a corral where several horses were bunched together near the shed wall. He called across the distance, and a brown stallion reared its head and ran toward the fence. The dogs worked under the rail and nipped at the large animal's feet. Cloyd hushed them with a snap of his fingers, sending them off to the barn. They slunk away with their tails between their legs.

"This is Roman. He's an old fellow; worked for many years for me. He'll do for you to learn the business on."

"Thank you, sir. Then you know him well." Jacky looked at the animal appraisingly. He was big.

"I raised him from a colt; the heir of a great stallion I had when I first came to the area and a dame I bought at an auction sale in those days when I was a dude like you."

"You didn't grow up here?" That surprised the boy.

"I was a young man when I chose to live in the West instead of the city like your parents. I always was more comfortable in the wide-open spaces than trapped in a court room like my old man. I hated the law; but it was his life, and I respected his choice as he finally accepted mine. Your grandmother was a gentle, refined woman, and I suspect your mother takes from her. I haven't seen her in years, but we've kept up a correspondence." As he was speaking, he led the horse and Jacky from the corral to the fence, where he left the horse, gathered up saddle, blanket and gear and prepared the boy for a ride.

Jacky was nervous. The horse stood calmly and quietly, but Jacky had never been expected to ride on the back of a large animal before. He had driven wagons and a carriage in town, but others had done the task of hitching and caring for the animals. He listened attentively to his uncle's instructions and patted the horse's nose and withers gently, then with a grip of iron and legs that quivered in fear, he swung his leg over the saddle and sat, his heart beating like a drum and his face hot with anxiety.

"Boy, when you ride, there's only one boss. You make sure your'n it. Give him too much lead, and he'll be gone to his feed." His uncle then stepped back, and Jackson Humboldt, the scholar and rebellious youth from Chicago, found himself alone on an animal, who stood stiff and unyielding. He used his voice, his heels and his hands on the reins to encourage the animal, but he wouldn't budge. He looked at Cloyd with a question in his eyes, and his uncle stepped to the horse, gave him a slap on the rear, and Jacky was thrown from the back of the beast and ignominiously landed in the manure-laced dirt of the farmyard. He coughed from the dust and picked himself up, brushed at his trousers and glanced at his uncle, who had caught the reins of the horse and stood waiting.

"Sorry, Uncle. My grip wasn't firm on the reins." Jacky coughed and tried not to look the fool he felt he was.

"Ack, happens to everyone from time to time. There's nothing to do but try again." His uncle patted the horse's nose and offered Jacky the reins.

And, again and again, Jacky thought, until his uncle called a halt for the day, saying he could have another try tomorrow. Cloyd demanded that Jacky unsaddle the uncooperative animal, curry him and lead him back to the corral and release him with the other horses.

"The poor beast can't wear the saddle just because you don't have the skill to remove it. Now, uncinch the animal's belly, and then we'll work on the bridle." Cloyd held one hand on the saddle horn to steady it as Jacky worked the straps loose.

The saddle was surprisingly heavy. Even taking it off the brute was hard work. The animal tired of his amateurish bungling, and by the time the bridle was loose and Jacky worked it off the animal's face, the horse fought him, making it even more difficult. He stored the saddle under his uncle's guidance and limped into the house. He felt a complete failure, and his back and legs seemed to belong to someone else, the pain was so dreadful.

Tommy was in the kitchen when Jacky came through the door, snapping peas at the table. "Are you ready for a lesson?" he asked her, partly hoping she would say no.

"Please." She smiled, and her face changed from somber to pleasant to look at.

"Let me clean up and we can start then." He smiled at her, even though he didn't feel it. He'd seen how his mother lit up when his father, even tired, said a kind word to her. He was pleased to see Tommy's smile grow wider.

After a good scrub at the kitchen sink, and a fresh shirt from his suitcase, Jacky took one of his dime novels, the one about the thief who was stealing children, and even though he thought it not quite appropriate for a lady's taste, he sat down with paper and pencil and began to teach Tommy how to read. She set her peas aside, pushing them to the back of the table, and with hungry eyes, followed along with each thing her young nephew showed her. Each simple letter of the alphabet was discussed and practiced until she told him she had to finish her peas and start on the evening's meal.

Over the next week, Jacky learned how to saddle his horse, ride with some success, and unsaddle the animal each afternoon. He found it simple to milk a cow, but not so easy to keep from being kicked if he was too aggressive. He broke a rotten egg, causing his uncle to laugh, and finally laughing himself. When the men returned each night from their work with the cattle in the fields, he hoped they saw he was more familiar with the ranch and how to do the various jobs around the barn. He greeted them with respect, but suspected all they heard was arrogance.

That all changed the night of the storm. The weather was heavy all day, and as the men rode out in the morning, Cloyd called Edmondson to the porch, advising him that should the clouds build into a true storm, he was to bring the horses in early. No sense in having them break a leg for a few cattle. Edmondson hadn't liked the admonition, but truth be told, the horizon was already turning gray by the time the men rode out of sight. The rain hit after lunch, and by the afternoon, lightning strafed the sky. Jacky and his uncle were in the barn currying Jacky's horse when an especially loud crack of thunder came just as a flash of lighting filled the inside of the barn. A portion of the roof shattered, sending wooden shingles showering inside. The horse bolted through the open door and into the storm. Flames licked the damage.

"Uncle! Roman's gone!" Jacky was in a panic, first from the noise, then from his horse bolting into the driving rain.

"As the barn will be, if we don't take care of that." Cloyd pointed to the flames. Bales of hay were piled under the opening, and his message was clear. If they caught, the entire barn would go up.

"The water buckets," Jacky yelled. Without further instructions, he grabbed the first one and clambered up the hay, tossing it at a place where a flaming piece of shingle had fallen into the hay. It sizzled before going out. He turned to find his uncle halfway up the stack with two more buckets. Three more buckets, and with the help of the pouring rain, the barn was safe.

Jacky could hardly hold still for wanting to find Roman.

"Leave it, boy. He's not my most valuable animal."

"He's my responsibility, Uncle. I have to get him." He pleaded, with tears flooding his soot-covered face.

"Then you must do it right." Uncle pulled a slicker from a peg and gave his nephew a lantern with a metal shield to keep the flame dry. He suggested the boy look first by the windmill, then, if not there, to try the field by the stand of willows.

When the ranch hands returned, the storm still raged, but Roman was in his stall under a blanket, Jacky was on a stool without his shirt and drying his hair with a horse blanket, and Cloyd was rigging a cover over his hay to keep it from being ruined. As the hands shook water off their hats and removed their trench coats to hang them to dry, Cloyd told the story of the boy who saved the barn, his horse, and possibly the entire ranch from total destruction.

As he became more accustomed to the traditions and customs of the western land, Jacky took on more responsibility and work, being guided by his uncle and aunt, who seemed to blossom before his eyes into a caring, lovely lady. As his uncle and the other men taught him, he taught her the manners and precepts of his gentle mother; how to properly set the table for company; how to fold a napkin; how to broil a chicken; and how to sit and rise gracefully from a chair. The silence and disdain between the couple remained, and Jacky began to despair of their ever becoming like his parents, but he gave each a share of his time and efforts.

The first time he was allowed to go into town with the men, he headed straight for the general store, after sending the required funds to his parents. What he needed most, he thought, was a cigar.

The bell above the door clanged as he walked inside. No one was about, but there were goods for sale lining the walls. A bell was on the counter, and he tapped it, letting it ding three times before turning to look around and wait.

"May I help you?" A heavyset man wiping his hand on a cloth stepped through a curtain. He wiped the corner of his mouth before setting the cloth on a low table.

"Cigars?" Jacky put his shoulders back, trying to look secure in his question. He'd been forced to sneak them at home, and he felt he might be called out if he looked too young.

"Any particular brand?"

"Um, what do you have?" Jacky hadn't thought about that. He should have had one in mind as a favorite. Dang.

"Only two, I'm afraid. Cuesta-Reys and Goldsmith and Silver's 108s. Not much call for them this direction. Most men go for tobacco and papers." He pulled down two wooden boxes off a shelf and opened them.

"Which is the best value?" After some discussion of the various attributes of each, none of which meant much to Jacky, he purchased three of the 108 variety. Outside, he pulled his knife from his pocket, cut the end, and struck a match to light one.

But, strangely, when he took the first breath into his throat and lungs, he found he didn't need it at all. It was no longer a symbol of rebellion, since no one objected to his taste in tobacco. He gave the other two to his uncle and learned to play poker with the ranch hands instead, cheerful whether he won or lost.

He was pleased to receive his first letter from home and devoured it with a new attitude. His father was still working, they had sold his boyhood home and most of the furniture and ornaments, and moved into a small two-bedroom house near the center of town, close to the street car terminal. They were comfortable and happy to receive news of their son so far away. A knot formed in his throat, and Jacky went out to sit on the stoop and gaze longingly toward the eastern sky. He shrugged his shoulders and went in for the nightly lesson with his aunt on addition and subtraction of numbers, while his uncle sat smoking in the corner, neither showing an interest or non-interest. Jacky, however, occasionally caught a smile cross his lips when his wife brightened at the wonder of learning a new word or fraction.

One morning in mid-June, Jacky strode out of the house following his uncle. He felt good about life in general, because he could now accept the many slurs on his person and character without taking them personally. He realized, after discussing it with Cloyd, that the hands treated all newcomers in the same manner. The sun was only a faint glimmer in the distance, rising slowly toward a horizon filled with deep crimson and dusky gray clouds that covered its brilliance, as it filled the darkness with light. He took a deep breath as he went up the steps of the bunkhouse and waited while Cloyd opened the door. The heat from the room hit him with a blow, as the scent of coffee, burned bread and bacon filled his nostrils. Cloyd walked to the table beside Edmondson and talked to him, while Jacky took his usual position along the wall. The men had stopped eating at their entrance. He heard a faint growl, and then the utensils moved and food was consumed again. He caught a quick glimpse of Edmondson as he nodded his head as if in agreement, and gently touched his glass with a spoon. The men stopped eating, and their heads came up as though birds perched on a wire.

Jacky's attention was only half on his uncle's instructions to his foremen and the other men. He anticipated going back to the far pasture on his horse and helping to round up stray cattle from the thickets and willows that grew along the gullies and side canyons, as he had done the last two days. He didn't mind the chore since he could now ride Roman without pain or discomfort. The old horse gave him self-confidence and an unfamiliar feeling of accomplishment. He hadn't yet acquired the skill of roping the cattle, so he just yelled and encouraged them to travel in the direction he had been instructed to send them.

Cloyd finished with a final, quiet gesture of farewell, since he and Tommy were going to visit the Wolcott family on the southern boundary of the ranch. They had talked at breakfast about the mutual need to separate the cattle that had strayed onto each other's property. He gave Jacky a nod as he went out the door, and Jacky raised a hand in acknowledgement.

Edmondson started giving orders to his men, and as they finished eating, they each rose and left the room. There was only a red-haired, freckled-faced man named Uriah and Jacky left. He hadn't worked near him before and didn't know him, except for his form and profile. Cornell collected a stack of dishes and left the room.

"Edkins, you and Humboldt take the wagon and wire and repair the fence along the line with the Wolcott ranch. We want no trouble with cattle straying back across the boundary once we get them separated. Don't attempt to catch or bother any Walcott brand you see; just keep a count and a location so the boys can round them up later. Humboldt, you'll need extra heavy gloves and the wire cutters. They're in the tool shed. Edkins, show him where, and hitch the team to the wagon. As soon as you get the wire and tools, Humboldt, join him, and the two of you get started. The boss and his missus will be going down the track toward the Wolcott place, so don't dawdle, but be aware that they're around."

Jacky turned to find the tools for mending fences and barely caught the sound of Edkins' complaints. He stood just outside the door, listening, as Edkins expressed his dismay and anger at having to wet nurse the dude all day. His nostrils flaring with resentment, Jacky moved down the steps and strode toward the tool shed. He had no idea what was needed to mend a fence. Edmondson had mentioned gloves and wire cutters, so he sorted among the many instruments on the table until he found what looked like wire cutters, a pair of pliers and a hammer, and picked up a wooden-handled post-hole digger. He knew what that was, for he'd seen men working on the street car line with them. He grabbed a pair of heavy-duty leather gloves, and pulled them on to see if they fit. They did, so he left them on while he carried the smaller tools to the cook shack and laid them on the porch. He saw that Edkins hadn't started hitching the wagon, so he went back for the post-hole digger. Coming out of the tool shed and closing the door behind him, he saw Edkins come riding out of the corral on a bay horse with no saddle. He stood stunned, holding the digger in his gloved hand and watched the dust cloud disappear toward town.

Edmondson came from the bunkhouse, his face pale and his eyes seemingly sunken in their sockets. He shook his head as though a fly had landed on his nose and marched down the step. "Alright, Humboldt, you're with me, today. Let's get the wagon hitched." He lifted his head and looked around. "It's going to be a hot one." And he walked to the corral, anger and pride in every step.

Jacky quickly put the post-hole digger near the other

tools and followed him, his curiosity at full-throttle, but he didn't dare ask a question. He caught one of the draft horses used for the wagons and led it out of the corral. He tied the horse's reins to the rail and watched as Edmondson led a matching horse out of the corral. He scrambled to latch the gate, for that was one of the first mistakes he'd made and never meant to make again, leaving the gate to the corral open, so horses or cattle could get out.

The two men, working in silent tandem, hitched the team and threw the tools in the back of the wagon. Edmondson hefted the heavy roll of wire onto the wagon bed and started to climb into the seat, but Jacky stopped him with a jerky movement of the hands.

"Ah, boss, did I get the right tools? I've never mended a fence before."

Edmondson stopped, one foot on the wagon wheel, prepared to board, and turned to Jacky as if he had forgotten the man was beside him.

"What?"

"The tools, did I pick the right ones?" Jacky could feel the sweat on his face and underarms as Edmondson examined the contents of the wagon bed.

He looked strangely at the younger man and replied, "You forgot the nails. They're in the lard can on the table; you know what nails look like?" he asked sarcastically.

Jacky scurried to fetch the nails. Holding the can tightly in his gloved hands, he put it in the wagon, hoping he'd chosen the right can. He climbed into the wagon seat and sat straight as a rod, as Edmondson drove out of the yard and across the grassy verge and onto a thin wagon trail across what seemed to Jacky miles of pasture. He could see cattle dotted on the plains, under the scanty trees and near the water tank. The sun was warm on his back, and he felt it penetrate the cloth of his shirt. The ground seemed to tilt, as the heat of the sun felt it would boil his brain; he pulled his hat lower on his head to help him concentrate.

"A fence is very important on a cattle or horse ranch, Jackson. Open government grazing land like this, all the cattle roamed freely, every rancher's herd straying for miles, seemed like. But, as the land was taken up by more settlers, and some of them not very friendly, the men began to use baling wire to keep the herds separate. Saves a lot of work and worry over the long haul. That's where the boss went today, to make sure the Wolcott ranch hands will know that Bar X Bar hands will be near their boundary in the next week. Don't want no shooting war to start among neighbors." He grinned, and Jacky felt more comfortable in his presence.

"Does that happen often, now?" He sure didn't want to get shot at by a stranger, thinking he was stealing cattle.

"Not in Wyoming, but over in Utah and New Mexico, it's been known. In the old days, lots of wealthy cattlemen got their start by branding a calf that didn't belong to him. It's been peaceful around here for many years." He seemed to withdraw into himself, and Jacky decided to leave him to his thoughts. He had a lot of his own, like, why didn't Uriah Edkins want to work with him? But, he didn't ask.

At last, when Jacky felt he would swoon from the heat and the steady clip, clip of the animals' hooves, he saw what looked like miles of wire stretched to the horizon.

"How do you know where the Wolcott boundary is?" He couldn't resist asking, for he saw nothing but the fence; the land on either side looked the same to him.

Edmondson drew the horses to a halt and laughed. "I suppose to a dude, it all looks alike, but those who've been here for years like me, we know every acre of land, every tree and creek. I don't suppose you'll be here that long." He laughed again, and Jacky turned in the wagon seat, offended, but didn't dare say so.

Edmondson slowly drove the wagon in a westerly direction, looking for cuts in the wire or downed fence posts. Twice he stopped and they strung new wire; twice Jacky felt the heat of the sun on his back and felt dizzy; but he drank water from a canteen, ate a couple of biscuits and a hunk of cheese from a basket. After a few more yards, Edmondson drove close to a place that looked wrong.

"There, boy, see the way the post is leaning, looks like the wire's holding it up." He stopped the wagon and climbed down, muttering to himself. He pulled a strong, four foot railroad post soaked with creosote from the wagon and tossed it on the ground. He reached for a machete, while Jacky dropped from the seat, his head swimming and sweat on his brow. He pulled the post-hole digger from the wagon and followed Edmondson.

The foreman leaned on the post and it gave way to his strength. It was rotted at the base and was held up solely by the wire attached to its surface. He picked up the machete and leaned forward to hack out some tall, blue-grey undergrowth that crowded out the place where he intended to dig.

At the first whack of the long knife, Jacky heard a hissing sound. He saw a large, black snake coiled not two feet from the foreman's boot tops. The man froze in fear.

Jacky stood with the hole-digger in his hands, his heart rate rising rapidly. He leaped high off the ground and brought the sharp blades on the bottom of the digger directly on the snake, slicing its head off; its jaw snapped as if still attached, while the headless body twisted and curled before finally lying lifeless on the grass. It was a bloody mess, and Jacky, now that the adrenalin had drained away, felt shaky and dizzy. He stared at the monster in shock.

Edmondson, his face wan and shiny with perspiration, went to the wagon and got the canteen, and without a word, handed the container to Jacky, who took a long drag of the tepid liquid and spit it on the ground. Edmondson took a cloth from his pocket, wet it with water from the canteen and offered it to Jacky to wipe his face and hands. He led the way back to the wagon, threw the tools and hole-digger into the back, and told him to climb aboard.

"Get in the wagon, Humboldt," he said gently to the boy, who stood motionlessly beside the wheel. He used his hand on Jacky's shoulder to urge him to obey. The boy swayed, but climbed into the wagon seat, his knees quivering with the suddenness of the snake attack.

Edmondson hopped into the driver's seat, released the brake and drove across the pasture, over the dry creek bed, and into the ranch yard.

Several men were sitting or standing under the shade trees near the bunkhouse wall, but they said nothing.

"Nils, you and Jake help Humboldt unload the wagon." Edmondson strode across the yard and knocked on the side door of the ranch house, and entered when bidden to do so.

Jacky, Nils and Jake Paulson unloaded the wire, the tools and the gloves, and put them back where they belonged. Jacky turned to Nils, "Thank you," he said quietly, but didn't elaborate. He walked to the back door to his room and collapsed on the bed, fully dressed, his head pounding from the day in the hot sun.

— 7 —

The long, endless days were filled with hard, boring work on some days and easy, sun-filled days of leisure as the men were allowed an occasional opportunity to go fishing or riding for pleasure. Jacky received a letter in late June that his father had gained most of his investments back from his loss of the winter, and Jackson was thrilled for his parents. His family had decided to remain living where they were, however, and that was accepted by him with a touch of amusement.

Jacky continued to work with Tommy to improve her reading skills, and she worked hard to better herself. She especially liked spending time in the Sears catalog. Seeing the pictures with the words helped her make the connection between the two, and the words stayed in her mind, she said. She spent hours totaling prices for various items she dreamed of around the house, then subtracting those that Cloyd might refuse to buy. She even began looking at women's clothes and dreamed of ordering something to surprise her husband. She seemed embarrassed when she told Jacky and made him promise not to tell.

Jacky noticed a subtle shift in attitude among the ranch

hands since the red-haired Uriah Edkins was no longer at the ranch. Especially, it seemed different at the dinner table at night. Cloyd no longer rose as soon as he ate and disappeared into the night wind. He began to tell stories of the old days, when as a young man, he'd first arrived in Wyoming. He told of the Indian tribes and of the long cattle drives up from Texas, and the drovers who'd brought the cattle and horses to the high plains. One night, without embarrassment, Tommy told of her father's beginnings and his struggle with the flooded river and the droughts and the day of the horrible locust plague. Jacky sat, enthralled by the tales, wide-eyed and alert. He told them of the tall buildings, the elevators and L trains that ran through the city, and of the lake that seemed as wide as an ocean.

His blistered hands healed and became callouses, his shoulders and legs were stronger, and he could ride almost all day without complaining. The cattle were branded and stood in pens waiting for the final count and a decision by the boss, whether to sell or release them back onto the pastures. The Wolcott family came for an overnight visit, and Tommy's friend, Sally Planter, and her sister, Thelma Muldoon, were frequent visitors, and when Jacky knew they were there, he made a hasty retreat to the bunkhouse, lest he get caught up in their feminine chatter. It proved that Sally was a middle-age matron with twinkling eyes and rosy cheeks, her once dark hair turned gray; and her sister, a widow with two children away in boarding school, seemed more somber, and dressed only in black or gray frocks. Tommy delighted in showing off her new skills, and the ladies pored over the articles and advertisements in the Sears catalog.

The first of July was welcomed by the inhabitants of the ranch with enthusiasm and anticipation despite the intensity of the dry heat and the blowing wind bringing dust to their eyes as they worked. Show bills began to appear in the windows of the local merchants and in the doctor's window. Pictures and descriptions of former rodeo events, and famous horses or bucking bulls of the past, enticed all to come see the spectacle and stay for the fireworks.

The men began to practice their riding and roping skills with industry and bragging, and Jackson Humboldt was no exception. He'd graduated from his awkward beginnings on the old, tired horse, Roman, to the more daring, thrilling run of the stallion, Gaither, who had gained his name from an old friend of Cloyd's who had ridden with him in his youth. The horse was a magnificent showman, and Jacky began to dream of a trophy to show his mother when he returned home.

But, no prize on the back of his horse could have pleased the boy more than the look on his uncle's face on the night before the Fourth of July races, when his aunt stood with poise and grace and read a poem from one of the books on the shelf. Jacky's heart raced with pride at her skill and daring, for the poem was a romantic one, and he anticipated a mellowing in their relationship.

Independence Day dawned hot and dry. All the old-timers were complaining of the lack of rainfall, and none grumbled more loudly than the ranch hands from the Bar X Bar. Nils was dressed in a blue shirt of finest cotton. Patches wore his red shirt and famous trousers with the patches on the knee and back pocket, for he would serve as a clown at the rodeo to be held in the afternoon. Jake and Thurman and the other hands were dressed in old, clean denims and scuffed boots, and Edmondson, his face freshly scrubbed and shaved, smelled of lilac water. The cook, Flapjack Cornell, was dressed in a dark suit of the finest wool, even on the hottest of days, and his hat perched atop his short, curly hair, for it was no secret that he was courting the widow Tate, who operated the local millinery shop.

Jackson Humboldt, dressed in his finest shirt and trousers, his new brown cowboy boots with the high heels neatly shined, waited until the last minute to leave his room, for he wanted to see the looks on the other men's faces when they saw their boss and his wife leave the house.

The horses were milling around, the men impatient to get to town for the excitement, as Jacky strode from the kitchen with the rush basket filled with food for their lunch tucked under his arm. The dogs were crazy with excitement, but they wouldn't be going, and they were ignored. Jacky placed the basket on the floor of the carriage and turned, his face solemn and sunburned from his days in the saddle and the harsh, blowing wind. The door opened, and a gasp rose from the waiting audience as Cloyd Fellows came forth, beaming from ear-to-ear, and gently holding the arm of his wife, Tommy Fellows, dressed in a new frock of palest blue, the collar teasing her chin, and the cuffs almost hidden under the soft white kid gloves on her hands. She held in one hand an unfurled, matching blue parasol with tiny, dangling white tassels around the rim, and her skirts swirling and switching around her black, patent leather boots.

Jacky was so excited, he thought his heart would burst inside his chest. He'd never seen her in a dress, and he imagined the other hands hadn't, either. The boss stepped lively down the steps, helping his wife as she followed, and he gently guided her into the carriage, circled the vehicle and took the reins. With a spring in his step, Jacky vaulted aboard and sat proudly as the residents of the Bar X Bar prepared to celebrate the day of Independence. He looked around as he rode into town. He loved his parents and his lifestyle in Chicago, but he couldn't imagine living anywhere else in the world. He knew his father would encourage him to return to Illinois for more education, but he'd come back, he promised himself. This vast open space had become his home, and he hoped to never leave it. He began to whistle a lively tune, and Tommy, his lovely aunt, turned and smiled.

He glanced to the side when Edmondson rode his horse close to the wagon. "Hey, boss," he yelled. "The dude thinks he'll beat me in the races. But, he'll never catch me." And he rode on down the lane, his crew following in a cloud of dust, their laughter echoing in the verdant grass.

Jacky yelled even louder, "Just wait and see, old timer; you'll be eating my dust before nightfall."

A great belly laugh and a soft, gentle chuckle were heard from the front seat, and Jackson Humboldt turned to laugh with them.

www.ingramcontent.com/pod-product-compliance
Lightning Source LLC
LaVergne TN
LVHW051829080426
835512LV00018B/2792